# A Resounding Tinkle

N. F. Simpson was born in London in 1919 and educated at Emanuel School and Birkbeck College. He served in the Royal Artillery and the Intelligence Corps during the Second World War, and then pursued a career in teaching and lecturing. He first achieved theatrical success as a winner of the Observer Play Competition with *A Resounding Tinkle* in 1957, and the play was staged at the Royal Court in the following year. It was followed by *The Hole* (1958), *One Way Pendulum* (1960), *The Form* (1961), *The Cresta Run* (1963) and *Was He Anyone?* (1972). Numerous contributions to West End revues, notably *One to Another* (1959) and *One Over the Eight* (1961), anticipated his subsequent success with shorter pieces for television, including the series *Three Rousing Tinkles* (1966), *Four Tall Tinkles* (1967), *World in Ferment* (1969), and *Charley's Grants* (1970). *One Way Pendulum* was filmed, starring Eric Sykes and George Cole, in 1964. From 1976 to 1978 he was Literary Manager of the English Stage Company at the Royal Court. A radio documentary about his life and work, *Reality is an Illusion Caused by Lack of N. F. Simpson*, was aired on BBC Radio 4 in April 2007. Now living in Cornwall, he continues to write, and his latest stage play, *If So Then Yes*, will be given a staged reading at the Royal Court in July 2007.

# N. F. SIMPSON

# A Resounding Tinkle

*and*

# Gladly Otherwise

*faber and faber*

*A Resounding Tinkle* first published
by Faber and Faber Limited in 1958

*Gladly Otherwise* first published
by Faber and Faber Limited in 1964
in *The Hole and Other Plays*

This edition first published in 2007
by Faber and Faber Limited
3 Queen Square, London WC1N 3AU

Typeset by Country Setting, Kingsdown, Kent CT14 8ES
Printed in England by CPI Antony Rowe

ISBN 978-0-571-23929-0

# Contents

*A Resounding Tinkle* exists in two published editions.

The one-act version staged at the Royal Court in 1957 and revived at the Donmar Warehouse in 2007 was published by Faber and Faber in 1964 in *The Hole and Other Plays* by N. F. Simpson.

The two-act version included in this volume was first published by Faber and Faber in 1958, and first staged in 1959 by Cambridge Theatre Actors, under the direction of John Bird, with Peter Cook and Eleanor Bron as Bro and Middie Paradock. A staged reading of this full version was performed at the Royal Court on 17 January 2006.

A Resounding Tinkle was first staged by the English Stage Company in the one-act version as a production without décor at the Royal Court Theatre, London, on 1 December 1957. It was revived in a double bill with *The Hole* on 2 April 1958. The cast was as follows:

**Bro Paradock** Nigel Davenport
**Middie Paradock** Wendy Craig
**First Comedian** Graham Crowden
**Second Comedian** Toke Townley
**Author** John Wood
**First Cleaner** Rita Webb
**Second Cleaner** Fanny Carby
**Technician** Leslie Glazer
**Producer** Patrick Barton
**American Tourist** Leslie Glazer
**Uncle Ted** Marigold Sharman

*Director* William Gaskill
*Designer* Tazeena Firth

**Gladly Otherwise** was first performed as part of the revue *One to Another*, which opened at the Lyric Theatre, Hammersmith, on 15 July 1959, and transferred to the Apollo Theatre, London, on 19 August 1959.

**The Man** Patrick Wymark
**Mrs Brandywine** Beryl Reid

*Director* Eleanor Fazan
*Designer* Disley Jones

**A Resounding Tinkle,** in the one-act version, and **Gladly Otherwise** were revived at the Donmar Warehouse, London, on 26 July 2007, in a triple bill with Michael Frayn's *The Crimson Hotel*. The cast, in order of speaking, was as follows:

A RESOUNDING TINKLE
**Middie Paradock** Judith Scott
**Bro Paradock** Peter Capaldi
**Uncle Ted** Lyndsey Marshal
**Voice of Vicar** John Hodgkinson

GLADLY OTHERWISE
**The Man** John Hodgkinson
**Mrs Brandywine** Judith Scott
**Mr Brandywine** Peter Capaldi

*Director* Douglas Hodge
*Designer* Vicki Mortimer
*Lighting Designer* Paule Constable
*Sound Designer* Carolyn Downing
*Composers* Stu Barker and Douglas Hodge
*Movement* Carolina Valdés

# A RESOUNDING TINKLE

# Characters

*Time: the present.*

### ACT ONE
*Scene One*
A suburban living room. Evening.

*Scene Two*
Same. Later the same evening.

### ACT TWO

Same. Evening next day.

# Act One

## SCENE ONE

*The living room. The silence between Bro Paradock, who stands with a glass in his hand looking out of the window, and his wife, Middie Paradock, whose glass stands beside her on the small table by which she is sitting, has clearly just fallen. It is not broken for nearly half a minute.*

**Mrs Paradock**  So don't flatter yourself.

*Bro Paradock turns from the window, empties his glass and, picking up Middie Paradock's glass, goes to a side table to fill both from one of two bottles containing a brightly purple liquid.*

**Mr Paradock**  I'm not flattering myself. And in any case we had all this out before.

**Mrs Paradock**  And now we're having it out again.

*Bro Paradock hands one of the two glasses to his wife. Both raise their glasses perfunctorily, grunt and sip. They are far from certain what to make of the bliss they come upon for the second time, and Bro Paradock, after another two sips, takes up the bottle and looks steadily at the label.*

**Mr Paradock**  I've never known this to happen before.

**Mrs Paradock**  It doesn't have to have happened before.

**Mr Paradock**  I can feel it hurrying through my veins like smoke.

**Mrs Paradock**  It's happened now. That's all you need concern yourself with.

**Mr Paradock** My lines seem to be coming to me in bits. Or what seem to be bits. This is like some unspecified milk of paradise.

**Mrs Paradock** What you can't remember you can make up.

**Mr Paradock** And what I can't make up can go unsaid.

**Mrs Paradock** No one minds with this kind of play. No one notices. You can be eight sheets in the wind or whatever it is practically from the word 'go' and the more the merrier from the author down. Or up. So don't for God's sake start having any qualms over remembering your lines or anybody else's lines. Just put it down to the ambrosia. Let ambrosia look after it.

**Mr Paradock** Ambrosia is what they eat. Not what they drink.

**Mrs Paradock** What who eat?

**Mr Paradock** You mean nectar. Let the nectar look after it. Not ambrosia.

**Mrs Paradock** Who said anything about nectar?

**Mr Paradock** You can't *drink* ambrosia, for God's sake! Ambrosia is the food of the immortals. It's what the gods eat.

**Mrs Paradock** I don't know what it is you're trying to prove with your slick emendations of every damn remark I make, but whatever it is you can go right ahead and prove something different.

*A knock.*

What the hell do you think you make me look like by comparison?

*Mrs Paradock goes out to answer the knock. Bro Paradock takes up a newspaper. Middie Paradock returns and begins tidying the room, speaking as she does so.*

There's somebody at the door wanting you to form a government.

*Bro Paradock looks at her in astonishment. Several seconds elapse.*

**Mr Paradock** What does he look like?

**Mrs Paradock** He says he's working through the street directory.

*Pause.*

I shall want this cork opened in case we have to offer him a drink. (*Pause.*) He was wearing an old raincoat. He looked as if he was trying it on for size.

**Mr Paradock** Give me the bottle. You can't open a cork. You should know that. You open the bottle. (*He begins to remove the cork.*) If it's an old raincoat what would he be trying it on for?

**Mrs Paradock** It might not be as old as the one he had before.

**Mr Paradock** I don't know why you wanted this bottle opened when the other one's more than half full.

**Mrs Paradock** The coat he had before may have been in tatters. It may have been black with grease. Or mud.

*With a preoccupied air, Bro Paradock takes a pipe from the mantelpiece and begins filling it.*

**Mr Paradock** How can I start forming a government at six o'clock in the evening?

**Mrs Paradock** You'd be saying the same thing if it were six o'clock in the morning.

*She takes a torn and dirty raincoat from a cupboard.*

Look at this thing. How do you know his mightn't have been in a worse state than this one? Look at the sleeves. And the collar – look at it. His was probably as bad or worse.

**Mr Paradock**  It's the Prime Minister's job.

**Mrs Paradock**  Oh yes. If you want to shelve your responsibilities I dare say it is the Prime Minister's job.

**Mr Paradock**  It's no concern of mine at all.

**Mrs Paradock**  There's a man at the door waiting for your answer.

*Pause.*

**Mr Paradock**  How do you know he isn't wanted by the police?

**Mrs Paradock**  Why should he be?

**Mr Paradock**  If he is, we ought to turn him over.

**Mrs Paradock**  If he's a criminal, he's in plain clothes – that's all I can say.

**Mr Paradock**  I'm going to turn him over.

*He moves to the door.*

**Mrs Paradock**  You may never get another chance to form a government.

**Mr Paradock**  That goes for anything I ever choose not to do.

**Mrs Paradock**  So what's it to be?

**Mr Paradock**  I'll see what he looks like.

*He goes out. Middie Paradock clears the table, sets out paper, ashtrays, water and glasses as for a board meeting.*

*Bro Paradock returns, takes up a newspaper and sits down in silence. Pause.*

It was Uncle Ted having a joke.

**Mrs Paradock**  I would have recognised him.

**Mr Paradock**  He was disguising his voice. He said I looked like Gladstone.

**Mrs Paradock**  And did you?

**Mr Paradock**  He wanted me to be taken in – I could see that.

**Mrs Paradock**  So I suppose you obliged?

**Mr Paradock**  That sort of thing cuts no ice with me.

**Mrs Paradock**  You should have led him on by pretending to think it was 1868.

**Mr Paradock**  It was all of a piece with his asking me to form a government.

**Mrs Paradock**  I hope you didn't start saying: 'My mission is to pacify Ireland'?

**Mr Paradock**  It cut no more ice with me than Gladstone would have done if I'd been Queen Victoria. And God knows there's little enough of the Empress of India about me.

**Mrs Paradock**  It would have been playing into his hands to say: 'My mission is to pacify Ireland.'

**Mr Paradock**  I know it would have been playing into his hands.

**Mrs Paradock**  I can't think why I didn't recognise him.

**Mr Paradock**  He said he was round canvassing for the Whigs.

**Mrs Paradock** Surely Uncle Ted knows you've never been a Whig?

**Mr Paradock** I suppose he thought he could talk me round like last time, when he had me voting for some candidate who refused to stand.

**Mrs Paradock** You should have let him come in for a few minutes to try your overcoat on.

**Mr Paradock** My overcoat would never fit Uncle Ted. Uncle Ted is broader across the shoulders than I am.

**Mrs Paradock** Exactly.

**Mr Paradock** He's a bigger man altogether than I am. He'd never get into my overcoat. I doubt whether he could even wear it like a cloak.

**Mrs Paradock** You don't see what I'm leading up to, do you? I know your overcoat is too small for him. It's too small for you except when you're in one of your pint-size moods. But if he'd tried it on I could have seen at a glance he wasn't a man of your build. I might after a time have been able to narrow it down to Uncle Ted. As it is, I don't know what to think.

**Mr Paradock** I've already told you it was Uncle Ted having a joke with us. It's just the kind of joke Uncle Ted would think up.

**Mrs Paradock** And what happened about the government? Did you agree to form one or not?

**Mr Paradock** I wasn't approached.

**Mrs Paradock** That's a likely story.

**Mr Paradock** He probably forgot.

**Mrs Paradock** If he forgot, how do you know it was Uncle Ted? It looks to me as if you've let yourself in for something with your bland assumptions about it being

Uncle Ted having a joke with us. You'll be getting somebody round before you know where you are with papers to prove it's 1868.

**Mr Paradock**  But not that I'm Gladstone.

**Mrs Paradock**  If it's 1868 it makes precious little difference whether you're Gladstone or Disraeli.

*A knock.*

**Mr Paradock**  Tell them I'm in conference.

**Mrs Paradock**  It'll be the concert party, I expect.

*Middie Paradock goes out. Bro Paradock sits down at the head of the table as though presiding at a directors' meeting of four, whose names around the table, anti-clockwise from himself, are Black, Green, White and Brown. Bro Paradock appears to be following a discussion which is passing back and forth across the table. Occasionally he intervenes to clarify a point, to invite a comment or to call someone to order. Middie Paradock returns.*

I've sent them upstairs to get their make-up on. It's the concert party.

**Mr Paradock**  Where are they going to do their act? There's no room in here for them.

**Mrs Paradock**  It doesn't last more than ten minutes or so.

**Mr Paradock**  They've still got to have somewhere to do it.

**Mrs Paradock**  They can do it in the room next door. We can watch through the serving hatch there. We've done it before.

**Mr Paradock**  (*shrugs*) As long as they're satisfied. Give me a hand to get this board meeting out of the way before they come down, Middie.

**Mrs Paradock** If I can find my shorthand.

*Middie Paradock fetches a notebook and pencil, quickly tidies her hair as she passes a mirror, puts on stylishly elegant spectacles and sits down beside Bro Paradock. The mime continues for a few moments, and Bro Paradock then rises to close the meeting.*

**Mr Paradock** Gentlemen. We have several proposals before us. I think we have three, to be exact – unless Mr Black's last point is to be taken as expanding the total to three and a half! (*He acknowledges laughter.*) The question is whether by continuing the meeting for another three or four hours we can reduce those three – and a half – proposals to one, or whether it would be better to congratulate ourselves on the progress we have already made and postpone a final decision for later consideration. As you know, gentlemen, and it is a melancholy thought – whatever we may decide, whatever plans we may make for the future of the company, it is beyond any of us to predict the conditions under which those plans will have to work, since no one can forecast – and perhaps least of all the government itself – what the government's future policy towards typewriter ribbons is to be. (*He acknowledges laughter*) We have cleared a great deal of useful ground here this afternoon, and I think you will agree with me when I say . . .

*First Comedian, wearing a white coat and carrying a stethoscope, enters.*

**Mrs Paradock** Here they are.

**First Comedian** The other one's coming in a moment. Where would you like us?

**Mrs Paradock** (*opening the door right into an adjoining room*) We thought perhaps in here would be rather nice.

*Middie Paradock leads First Comedian out, switching on the light to reveal a small adjoining room containing a washbasin, a light, long wooden table and a desk. Bro Paradock puts his head through the hatch.*

**Mrs Paradock** We haven't got a stage for you, I'm afraid, but there's any amount of hot water upstairs if you want to wash the make-up off afterwards.

**Mr Paradock** We thought for the moment you were Uncle Ted back.

**Mrs Paradock** We thought nothing of the kind. He thinks it's 1868 and you've come to ask him to form a government. It's all he ever thinks about.

**First Comedian** I'd like an old blanket on this table, Mrs Paradock, and two or three cushions if you could manage it.

**Mrs Paradock** I can manage the blanket; I'll see what I can find for you to use as cushions.

**First Comedian** A pillow would do. I only want to prop his head up.

**Mrs Paradock** I'll find something. And say nothing to him whatever you do about Edward Cardwell. He's only waiting for a chance to have you reforming the Army. He thinks he's Gladstone.

**Mr Paradock** I'm not deaf and I don't need humouring, thank you.

**Mrs Paradock** Cushions and a blanket.

*Middie Paradock goes out.*

**Mr Paradock** There's plenty of hot water in the bathroom upstairs.

*First Comedian continues in silence to set his scene, placing the table near the front of the stage and*

*arranging papers on the desk. Middie Paradock comes
in with blanket and cushions.*

I was telling our friend here there's plenty of hot water
upstairs if they want it afterwards.

**Mrs Paradock**  A spotlight would be more to the point.
They can't do their act in total darkness.

**Mr Paradock**  It isn't what they can do that matters. Or
what they can't do. It's what we can see them doing.
That's the thing that matters.

*First Comedian places cushions under the blanket,
with which he covers the table to form an improvised
couch as for a doctor's patient.*

**First Comedian**  I think we're about ready now, if you
wouldn't mind giving my friend a shout. He can come
through the same door there when you've put out the
light in your room.

**Mrs Paradock**  Do you hear that, Bro? We're to have our
light out. You'd better have your torch ready.

*Middie Paradock goes out and returns almost
immediately.*

He's just coming down. Where's your torch, Bro, before
I switch out the light?

**Mr Paradock**  It's here ready. I've had it ready all the time
while you've been talking.

**Mrs Paradock**  Isn't this exciting?

*She switches off the light. By the light of the torch she
finds her way to the hatch. First Comedian is sitting at
his improvised desk, writing. He leans forward, presses
a button, and says 'Ping'. The door from the living
room opens to admit a man of no particular age
between forty and sixty, whose nondescript appearance*

*and defeated air contrast with the brisk, ebullient manner the First Comedian has assumed. This is the Second Comedian. He approaches the desk and sits diffidently down. When after a few minutes the First Comedian disengages his attention from what he is writing, the Second Comedian leans forward.*

**Second Comedian** It's my feet, Doctor.

**First Comedian** What's the matter with your feet?

**Second Comedian** I was rather hoping you might be able to tell me that, Doctor.

**First Comedian** Let me see them.

*Second Comedian takes off shoes and socks.*

**Second Comedian** They're all right now. It's when they suddenly swivel round they catch me.

*Second Comedian holds out both legs quite straight in front of him. First Comedian stands over them.*

**First Comedian** What are these?

**Second Comedian** They're my kneecaps, Doctor.

**First Comedian** They ought to be much higher up your legs than this.

**Second Comedian** I can't seem to keep them up, Doctor.

**First Comedian** Take everything off except your trousers and lie down over there.

*First Comedian goes to washbasin, where he begins washing his hands, while Second Comedian goes into the corner, where the desk conceals him, to undress.*

Eardrums still getting overheated?

**Second Comedian** Only when I listen to anything, Doctor.

*Second Comedian comes out and lies down on the couch. First Comedian examines his chest.*

**First Comedian** Breathe in deeply. Again. Yes – you're having trouble with your breathing. Breathe out. Do you notice any difference?

**Second Comedian** None at all, Doctor.

**First Comedian** And do you know why? The reason you notice no difference is that there isn't any. All the time while you're breathing out, there's air forcing its way in. It's trying to push past. Breathe in again. (*He reflects for a moment.*) Do you ever feel as though the air you're getting is the wrong kind of air?

**Second Comedian** I just don't get the air, Doctor.

**First Comedian** Somebody must have it if you don't.

**Second Comedian** It's my lungs, Doctor.

**First Comedian** Nonsense. There's nothing wrong with your lungs. They're both perfectly fit.

**Second Comedian** I don't think they hit it off, Doctor. They're at daggers drawn practically the whole time. Over the air.

**First Comedian** And your breathing's twisted to blazes as a result. Let me see your tongue. Open your mouth. (*He looks inside*) You've had this jaw to pieces, haven't you?

**Second Comedian** It was some years ago, Doctor.

**First Comedian** It doesn't matter how long ago it was. It's not a question of time. You laymen start dismantling these parts, but you've no idea how to put them together again. Here's a tooth which has been put back upside down. You're biting on the root.

*First Comedian begins to use the stethoscope.*

**Second Comedian** I've been told I can expect all my teeth to turn turtle eventually.

**First Comedian** What are you doing about it?

**Second Comedian** Consulting you, Doctor.

**First Comedian** I thought you'd come to me about your feet.

> *First Comedian grimaces as he continues to sound Second Comedian's chest.*

What on earth are you carrying round in this bloodstream of yours?

**Second Comedian** Only my blood, Doctor.

**First Comedian** You've got a hell of a noisy circulation.

**Second Comedian** I have, Doctor. It keeps me awake.

**First Comedian** I should think so. It sounds like a mobile iron foundry. You need a silencer for it. I'll give you a letter to take to the King's Cross Blood, Brain and Bowel Hospital. You can have it under the National Health.

**Second Comedian** I'd like them to look at my arteries while I'm there as well, Doctor. They seem to have venous blood in them.

**First Comedian** It's when you get arterial blood in the veins that you need to begin worrying. Turn over and let me look at your back.

> *Second Comedian turns painfully over and First Comedian stands looking for some moments in silence.*

**Second Comedian** I've had it some time, Doctor.

**First Comedian** I can see that. And we can write off these kidneys.

**Second Comedian** I hardly ever use them, Doctor.

**First Comedian** How long have your ribs been like this?

**Second Comedian** As long as I can remember, Doctor.

**First Comedian** And how long is that? Months? Years?

**Second Comedian** I can't altogether recall, Doctor.

*First Comedian goes back to his desk where he takes up a pen and begins writing briskly.*

**First Comedian** You can get your clothes on.

*While Second Comedian gets dressed, First Comedian goes on writing. When Second Comedian reappears, he puts down his pen.*

Sit down, Mr Avalanche.

*Second Comedian sits down hesitantly and waits for First Comedian to begin.*

I don't suppose there's much I can tell you that you don't know already. It's an obsolete body, of course, as you realise. And I'm afraid you'll have to do the best you can with it. You must learn to co-operate with your organs.

**Second Comedian** The small of my back is too big, Doctor.

**First Comedian** There's nothing to be gained by pretending it isn't. In fact I'll be quite frank with you, Mr Avalanche – it's a great deal larger than it should be. Not only in your case, but with a surprisingly large number of people. But there's absolutely no need for you to have any misgivings about it. People go on – some of them with far less wrong with them than you have by a long way – they go on living active lives sometimes for years. There's no reason at all, Mr Avalanche, why given time you shouldn't have a good twenty or thirty years in front of you.

**Second Comedian** With a transparent pelvis, Doctor?

**First Comedian** The main thing is to keep that blood circulating. Take precautions, but don't overdo it. Sleep whenever you can with your eyes closed. Keep off strong poisons of all kinds – and breathe. Breathe all the time. If it doesn't seem to be showing results, make sure it isn't because you're under water. Keep at it: the more you breathe the better you'll feel.

**Second Comedian** I've been having a lot of trouble with my slanting bowel since I became allergic to smells, Doctor.

**First Comedian** You will for a time, but it's nothing to worry about. Take this letter to the Blood, Brain and Bowel Hospital and they'll give you a thorough overhaul.

**Second Comedian** I shall feel a lot easier, Doctor.

**First Comedian** And get those feet seen to. They'll be no good to you while they swivel. You should be seeing somebody about them. The feet should never swivel. Hand that letter in to the almoner and you can come back here when the specialist has seen you.

**Second Comedian** Thank you, Doctor. And I'll come in again, as you say, when I've been examined.

**First Comedian** Next Thursday. I can't see you before then. And I'll give you something for those elbows to see if we can't get them bending the right way.

**Second Comedian** Very good, Doctor.

*Second Comedian goes listlessly out, switching off the light as he does so. As he enters the living room, he switches that light on. Bro and Middie Paradock withdraw from the hatch and close it. Middie Paradock half opens the door into the passage through which the Second Comedian has gone.*

**Mrs Paradock**  You can find your own way upstairs, I expect. You'll find plenty of hot water up there.

*She closes the door.*

**Mr Paradock**  It's Aunt Chloe's birthday next week.

**Mrs Paradock**  So you keep saying.

**Mr Paradock**  We shall have to think of something.

**Mrs Paradock**  Unless we send Doris round when she comes home from school?

**Mr Paradock**  There's never anything she wants. If you think of anything, she's always got it. Everything you think of she's got already.

**Mrs Paradock**  Listen. Hear them? Hear them washing their make-up off upstairs?

**Mr Paradock**  What's the good of sending Doris round?

**Mrs Paradock**  Not if she were to burst a paper bag in Aunt Chloe's ear? We could get her a deaf aid.

**Mr Paradock**  I don't see why we should go to all that trouble. It isn't as if it's her twenty-first.

**Mrs Paradock**  I thought that was rather novel when he said: 'You've had this jaw to pieces.'

**Mr Paradock**  I was expecting him to make some remark about dry rot in the roof of his mouth.

**Mrs Paradock**  It was very unpredictable.

**Mr Paradock**  Except at the end. That bit about the elbows bending the wrong way. I could see that coming.

**Mrs Paradock**  That wasn't till right at the end.

**Mr Paradock**  I could see it coming.

**Mrs Paradock**  You mean you think you could see it coming. You're being wise after the event again. If you could see it coming why didn't you say so before it came? That would have been the time to say it instead of waiting till it was all over.

**Mr Paradock**  Because if I'd said so before it came, it would have spoiled it for you.

**Mrs Paradock**  How did you know I hadn't seen it coming myself?

**Mr Paradock**  Because you'd have said so.

**Mrs Paradock**  And spoiled it for you?

**Mr Paradock**  You wouldn't have spoiled it for me because I saw it coming all along, as you well knew.

**Mrs Paradock**  One of these days you'll be wise after the event once too often. Did we give them supper last time?

**Mr Paradock**  We've never had them before.

**Mrs Paradock**  We would never have had them this time if it had been left to you. You'd better ask them what they want to drink when they come down.

*Bro Paradock goes to the table behind the door, where he is unseen at first by the two comedians, who enter, wearing dark lounge suits, as Middie Paradock goes out.*

Here they are. There'll be something ready for you in a few minutes if you'll excuse me while I get it served up.

*She closes the door behind her.*

**First Comedian**  I thought they were going to send us off without anything.

*They catch sight of Bro Paradock. A difficult pause.*

**Mr Paradock**  You'd like a drink, I expect. I'll get you some clean glasses.

*Second Comedian opens the door and closes it behind Bro Paradock, who goes out with the tray. First Comedian shrugs, picks up a magazine, and sits with his back to the audience.*

**Second Comedian** You're being a bit casual, aren't you? What about all these people?

**First Comedian** Well?

**Second Comedian** We can't sit down and read magazines.

**First Comedian** It's not my job to spoon-feed them.

**Second Comedian** They'll get restive.

**First Comedian** Let them talk among themselves for a time.

*Second Comedian sits doubtfully down with a magazine, but is increasingly ill at ease. He gives up the effort to read and, standing up, looks across to the First Comedian. Convulsively he turns and makes an agonised attempt to address the audience direct.*

**Second Comedian** (*inarticulate for a few moments*) Good people . . .

*He can get no further and turns angrily on First Comedian, who is now watching him with interest.*

Don't just sit there!

**First Comedian** (*putting down his magazine*) Now listen to me, Bug. Just take it easy, will you? Sit down and take that look off your face. Give it to a rabbit to wear when it meets a stoat. You look like death.

*Miserably, Second Comedian sits down.*

**Second Comedian** Maybe it isn't your job to spoon-feed them. But it's not mine either.

**First Comedian**  Then we can both stop worrying. If they don't want to amuse themselves they can make do with silence.

**Second Comedian**  They'll never stand for it.

**First Comedian**  We can break it up with dialogue from time to time if it would make you any easier. And silence isn't so easy to come by as all that, either, if it comes to that.

**Second Comedian**  It's not what you go to a theatre for. You go to other places for silence. Not a theatre. They'll feel cheated.

**First Comedian**  It's possible. I've known people feel cheated about some odd things. I've known people buy a bath sponge and do calculations to show that two-thirds of the sponge is made up of holes. And it galls them to think that two-thirds of what they've paid good money for isn't really there. Of course they feel cheated. They have every right to feel cheated. They've been overcharged. They've been overcharged two hundred per cent.

**Second Comedian**  Not with a sponge. They've no right to feel cheated over a sponge. A sponge is where you expect to find holes. But a theatre is not where you expect to find silence. That's the difference. The holes are there for a purpose in a sponge. They're there to soak up the water.

**First Comedian**  Now you're bringing a new element into it. Start talking about purpose and you'll have the whole argument bedevilled. Before we know where we are, we shall be splitting hairs. No. Leave purpose out of it. They're not there *to* soak up the water. The holes in a sponge soak up the water. It's not the same.

**Second Comedian**  Which is what I said in the first place. The holes are there for a purpose.

**First Comedian** Purpose, purpose, purpose! It isn't purpose – it's coincidence! They happen to be there and they happen to soak up the water. The holes were there long before you or anybody else ever used a sponge in a bath. And that goes for everything else. It goes for sponges and it goes for . . . for everything else. What, for instance, is the purpose of the sea? Is it so that sponges can have somewhere to grow? To give fish somewhere to use their gills? Perhaps you want to tell me that oceans exist to cater for submarines? Rather than waste all those submarines on dry land, God in His all-seeing wisdom made the sea. That's how you're arguing. You're arguing from effect back to cause and it's disastrous.

**Second Comedian** You're going too fast for me. Your mind doesn't work the way mine does. Let me come to it in my own way.

**First Comedian** Good God, we're going to be at it all night. Surely you can see the analogy with a sponge. We don't have to run a bath for you and let you get into it, do we? With your ducks and your boats, before you can see a simple analogy?

**Second Comedian** Offensive swine!

**First Comedian** All I'm trying to say is that anyone who starts with the idea of sponge, and starts squeezing water over himself out of it before he lets his mind wander slowly back through the millennia to the beginnings of things, is going the wrong way about it. He'll end up in a paroxysm of wonder. He'll want to start worshipping something, on the spot, while he's still dripping with water and his glasses are steamed up. And for no better reason, for no more compelling reason, than that the entire evolutionary processes of the cosmos seem to him to have been geared for several million years to the task of providing him with something to wash himself with.

How marvellous are Thy ways, O Lord! The seasons always working out just right for the crops; the flowers never forgetting what colour they have to be to attract the right kind of insect and repel the wrong kind, blessed be God! Isn't it wonderful the way it all works out? And if it had worked out quite differently that would have been pretty wonderful too.

**Second Comedian**  What none of this alters, or even begins to make any impression on as far as I can see, is the irrefutable fact that five minutes of dead silence, or even two or three minutes of it, is going to open the floodgates of their indignation like the bottom coming out of a bag of cement. They won't stomach it.

**First Comedian**  At the end of three or four minutes of silence, if it would put your mind at rest, we could have a hunting horn.

**Second Comedian**  Where would that get any of us?

**First Comedian**  Or a horse whinnying. To break the tension. Kettledrums. Anything like that.

**Second Comedian**  Bringing a neighing horse onto the stage is going to present us with more problems than it solves.

**First Comedian**  A whinnying horse. I said nothing about a neighing horse.

**Second Comedian**  People won't stand for it.

**First Comedian**  As for problems, of course a horse on the stage presents problems. Of course it does. And suppose we solve all the problems it presents? What happens? We end up with more problems than we started with. Because that's the way problems propagate their species. A problem left to itself dries up or goes rotten. But fertilise a problem with a solution – you'll hatch out dozens. It's better than breeding budgerigars. There isn't

25

anything very challenging about a budgerigar. There's a limit to what you can do by way of experiment. Horse-breeding and dog-breeding and all the other hobbies people have to occupy them when they're not breeding problems are not for you and me. The people who count are the ones who devote their lives to a search for the sterile solution from which no further problems can be bred. I hope they never find it. The moment they do, the world ends.

**Second Comedian**  Don't let my presence on the stage cramp your style. Go on as if I weren't here. Make a full-blooded soliloquy of it while you're in voice. Open the hatches and disgorge. Give us all plenty to flounder in and damned be him that first cries, 'Hold, enough!' Only count me out.

*As Second Comedian makes to fling open the door, Middie Paradock enters, carrying a tray of food.*

**Mrs Paradock**  Oh.

*She pauses uncertainly, and then goes to the table to put down the tray.*

I hope I haven't interrupted you both in the middle of a quarrel.

*Bro Paradock enters with a tray of drinks, which he puts down on the small table behind the door.*

**Mr Paradock**  You'd like an aperient I expect.

**Mrs Paradock**  Put it down and leave it. They can pour their own in a moment.

**Mr Paradock**  Oh.

*Middie Paradock takes Bro Paradock aside.*

**Mrs Paradock**  We've come in at the wrong moment. They were about to have a set-to.

*They go towards the door.*

**Mr Paradock**  Is there anything you need? Or can you manage?

**Mrs Paradock**  Of course they don't need anything. There are knives in the drawer if they want to go at each other in that way.

*Bro and Middie Paradock go out and close the door. Second Comedian goes to the small table, where he pours out two glasses of the purple drink and brings them to the larger table on which First Comedian has set out the food. They sit and begin their meal, eating and drinking for some time in silence.*

**Second Comedian**  (*holding up his glass*) This is like the milk of paradise.

*They continue to eat in silence.*

It'll save time if we test for humour now.

**First Comedian**  Afterwards.

**Second Comedian**  Where I get baffled is over isolating the quintessential comic element.

*Pause.*

You could get rid of the linguistic overtones by using Esperanto, but that means evening classes for comedian and audience alike while they're all learning Esperanto.

**First Comedian**  They might not like the joke any more in Esperanto than they did in English.

**Second Comedian**  And after months of part-time study they'd be in a pretty ugly mood.

**First Comedian**  It's the wrong approach altogether. If you want to isolate the quintessential comic element, the only way you can do it is through your laughter response index.

**Second Comedian** You mean through my own, personal laughter response index? Because if so there's nothing doing there. Every joke I've ever thought of has been tried out on myself first.

**First Comedian** And what's your laughter response index?

**Second Comedian** I get a nil reading. I've got no sense of humour.

**First Comedian** I doubt that. You may have a low laughter quotient. Many people have. But it's ridiculous for a comedian to be without a sense of humour altogether.

**Second Comedian** I keep it under control. I like to keep my satiric vision unimpaired.

**First Comedian** Satiric vision my sunglasses! You've got about as much satiric vision as a hawk with bifocals has got eyes like a lynx. Or vice versa, as far as that goes. You remind me of a lark walking the plank with its eyes closed. Slowly. Cautiously. Feeling its way step by step, making a false move and clutching convulsively at the air before hitting the water.

*They continue the meal in silence.*

You remind me of a pigeon coming down by parachute.

*Silence.*

Coming down by parachute because it likes to keep its neuroses airborne as long as possible.

**Second Comedian** You're as smug as a parrot.

**First Comedian** You remind me of a cormorant.

**Second Comedian** As smug as a parrot from the Azores. I only hope when you hit the water you don't find it frozen over. Or that if you do you're wearing your skates. If you're wearing your skates when you hit the water and find it frozen over, you can be as smug as you like till kingdom come and I wish you joy of it. Till then, leave it to the parrots, please.

**First Comedian** You remind me of a cormorant with a beak a yard long tapping out a manifesto to the cosmos on a second-hand typewriter. I affirm letter by tipsy letter that I exist! I am in revolt (with reservations) against revolt! I do not choose not to be! Beak first, it plunges like a kingfisher into the glutinous mud, sticks fast and quivers like a tuning fork.

*They eat the rest of their meal in silence and then, pushing back their chairs, get up from the table.*

I wonder what kind of an allegory they'll make of that.

**Second Comedian** We shall know soon enough.

*They move in an unsettled way about the room, picking up and putting down books and ornaments, looking out of the window, yawning.*

**First Comedian** I suggest we have one more drink and then see what we can do on the strength of it by way of getting the curtain down.

*He pours two drinks, one of which he hands to Second Comedian.*

Go for spontaneity. Just give the dialogue its head – it's bound to be almost played out by now.

**Second Comedian** This seems a damned hit-or-miss way to me of doing things.

**First Comedian** It won't when you've had some more nectar. Drink up. A sort of rallentando close should do it very nicely, but don't try to force it. Let it take its course.

*First Comedian takes up a position at the window.*

The stars are a long way off tonight.

*Second Comedian joins him for a moment at the
window, looks up as though to verify First Comedian's
observation and then turns away.*

**Second Comedian**  The planets are not much nearer.

*Second Comedian stands looking intently at a goldfish
in a bowl. First Comedian comes away from the
window.*

**First Comedian**  In 1751 Dr Joseph Priestley was
distressed that he could not feel a proper repentance for
the sin of Adam.

*Second Comedian continues to stare into the goldfish
bowl. First Comedian has something on his mind which
he is uncertain how best to put into words. He takes
up a position behind a high-backed chair as though in
front of a rostrum.*

**Second Comedian**  The open sea is a closed book to this
goldfish.

*Pause. Second Comedian turns away from the goldfish.*

**First Comedian**  I concede that the earth could be flat.
But I doubt it. I doubt it for a number of reasons which
I don't intend to go into now. I'd like to put it to the test.
I'd very much like to put the whole theory to the test
simply by sailing west as far as I could go. If my reckoning
is reliable, and if the earth is, as I believe, spherical, I ought
eventually, unless there happens to be other land in the
way, to arrive on the coast of China.

**Second Comedian**  It's a persuasive theory.

**First Comedian**  It opens up so many possibilities. Take
the sun. We talk about sunrise and sunset. How do we
know that what we imagine to be the sun rising and the
sun setting, and what we imagine to be the sun moving
from east to west across the sky, aren't all in fact a simple

30

optical illusion? How do we know that it isn't we who are moving, while the sun remains motionless in the heavens?

**Second Comedian**  I suppose anything could be an optical illusion.

**First Comedian**  Look at it this way. This is very tentative, but you've been in a train often enough, haven't you, when another train is drawn up alongside it. Now. One train begins to move. You can feel nothing, but you look through the window and decide that it's the other train which is moving backwards. As you gather speed, however, the movement of your own train as it begins to sway tells you that in fact it is you who are moving forwards.

**Second Comedian**  I think some of this has been gone into before.

**First Comedian**  You'd get exactly the same effect as you got with the trains if the earth were to be spinning in the opposite direction to the apparent movement of the sun across the sky.

**Second Comedian**  In fact there are a good many people who seem to organise their lives on some such assumption.

**First Comedian**  I don't intend to let this rest here. If Columbus was right on this score, he was very likely right on other things too. But no one will ever know what those other things were until someone takes the trouble to find out. And people aren't going to go to the trouble of finding out until he's been proved right on this point first. That's why it's up to me to vindicate him if I can. I'm certain he was right.

**Second Comedian**  He bides his time who's stuck knee-deep in lime.

**First Comedian**  I can't see what that's got to do with it.

**Second Comedian** It's a proverb.

**First Comedian** You seem to set precious little store by relevance, I must say.

**Second Comedian** I prefer to go off at a tangent.

**First Comedian** And damned smug you sound about it, too!

**Second Comedian** I stand for the line of least resistance.

**First Comedian** Then let's both doze off.

*They sit opposite each other and close their eyes. Both begin muttering under their breath. At last First Comedian opens his eyes suspiciously. Suspicion turns to anger, and, leaping up, he gestures violently to where Second Comedian is sitting bolt upright and with eyes now open.*

You cavalier bastard! You've been talking in my sleep!

**Second Comedian** How was I to know whose sleep it was?

**First Comedian** You could have asked, couldn't you?

**Second Comedian** What the hell!

**First Comedian** It was a pretty cavalier thing to do, that's all I'm saying. You might ask next time.

*Both subside. There is a pause. Second Comedian gets up from his chair.*

**Second Comedian** Not a year passes but I am older.

*Pause.*

**First Comedian** By how much I grow older, by so much am I nearer my end.

*Pause.*

**Second Comedian** When the end comes there is no more.

*Both look up at the curtain, which begins to fall very
slowly. They follow it down a short way with their
eyes, turn to look at each other in mutual search for
confirmation, find it and rush to pour themselves
another drink. They drink to success as the curtain
comes quickly down.*

### SCENE TWO

*In front of the curtain appears a man of perhaps thirty-
five, well dressed and easy mannered; he would pass
for a third-generation estate agent with an office in
Knightsbridge. He represents the author. He has a glass
in his hand, which is half full of a bright, purple liquid.*

**Author**  I agree. A pretty epileptic start. We're going to
see what we can do in the next scene about pulling the
thing together. Because this isn't at all of course how I
wrote the play. You must have realised that. We're all –
what shall I say? – we're all just a thought oiled over
on this side of the footlights. I expect you've gathered
that. And of course the thing was by no means as
straightforward as I could have wished even before this
crate arrived backstage. It really is remarkable stuff, I might
say. Milk of paradise is . . . well, it's not what I would
have called it, but I can see the connection; anyone
casting around for some phrase to just hit it off with,
might well seize on one like that. And of course one is
quite possibly not as clear-headed after two or three
glasses of this as to be able to explain altogether clearly
what it is one is trying to do. Conversely, as it were, such
an explanation would hardly have been needed had one
not failed – rather lamentably, I must admit – to achieve
what one was trying to achieve. How close we're getting
to the original tonight is anybody's guess – it would have
been anybody's guess whether this nectar had arrived so

unexpectedly or not. Because I know hardly a word of
Portuguese, and of course Portuguese is precisely the
language, unfortunately, in which the play – or most of
it – came to me. I was pretty much in the dark, I can tell
you, until I got to work with a dictionary. I had someone
help me, naturally, and between us we've hammered out
something, but I'm far from happy about the whole thing.
I think what you'd all better do is to visualise if you can a
regimental sergeant-major on a kitchen chair in the middle
of a bare stage with his back to you. He has a megaphone
through which quite suddenly he'll begin reciting Jabber-
wocky over and over again for three hours at top speed.
I want that image to be clear in your minds, and I want
you to hold it there throughout this performance of ours
tonight. It is our sheet anchor. Without that image in our
minds we shall lose all sense of proportion about what
we're going through here and now. For let us make no
mistake about it, we are in this together and we must do
what we can to see that no one of us suffers more than
another. There is no desire, no intention on my part,
or on the part of any of us on this side of the footlights,
to impose upon you any ready-made idea of our own as
to what this play ought to turn out to be. So often the
author – we have all known him – moves invisibly among
his audience nudging one and distracting another,
muttering and mouthing among his betters. Or he leans
forward from time to time to make simultaneous overtures
of sumptuous impropriety to every Aunt Edna in the house.
Such has never been my conception of the relationship
that should exist between us. No. It is together that we
must shape the experience which is the play we shall all
of us have shared. The actors are as much the audience
as the audience themselves, in precisely the same way
that the audience are as much the actors as the actors
themselves. We are all spectators of one another, mutual
witnesses of each other's discomfiture. Each of us as he

receives his private trouncings at the hands of fate is kept in good heart by the moth in his brother's parachute, and the scorpion in his neighbour's underwear. So let us in the name of that *Schadenfreude* that binds us each to each work from now on together, you on your side of the footlights, and we on ours. We shall need all you can give us. Dramatic situations, plot, glamour, spectacle, lyricism. And some tragic relief. And if we could possibly step up the intellectual content at all? Some of you these days are travelling in from places as far out as Harrow and Morden, and you just have to have your minds stimulated more than in the days when the illusion of thought had to last no farther than Hammersmith or Putney. So there it is. I'll go off now into the wings. We'll leave the stage quite empty for a moment or two, and I think that if, like Quakers, we all compose our minds in a kind of mystic amalgam, something may come of it.

*He goes off as the curtain rises on the living room as it was at the end of the first scene. The two comedians are sprawled, fast asleep, in armchairs. Bro and Middie Paradock have just come in.*

**Mrs Paradock** I'm not saying it's your fault.

**Mr Paradock** Not a drain.

**Mrs Paradock** I'm not saying it's your fault. All I'm saying is that to give them two bottles, both practically full, is hardly the best way to go about things if you want to conserve your nectar.

**Mr Paradock** They might have shown a bit more restraint than to swallow the lot. They call themselves comedians. I'd like to know what's supposed to be comic about drinking to excess.

**Mrs Paradock** They haven't got to be comic the whole time.

**Mr Paradock**  I wouldn't employ them to sell typewriter ribbons.

**Mrs Paradock**  Neither would anybody else while they were in that state.

**Mr Paradock**  It doesn't take you long to leap to their defence, I notice. I wonder if you'd find it so comic if I started drinking to excess.

**Mrs Paradock**  You've never done anything to excess in your life. That's just your trouble.

**Mr Paradock**  I happen to prefer moderation.

**Mrs Paradock**  You make a vice of it. You never know when not to stop.

**Mr Paradock**  I wouldn't employ them to sell typewriter ribbons for me.

**Mrs Paradock**  So you keep saying.

**Mr Paradock**  No more would I.

**Mrs Paradock**  And while you're not employing them selling typewriter ribbons other people are stealing a march on you in some other trade.

**Mr Paradock**  Comedians! I'd like to know what's comic about them now. Look at them. It isn't as if they're lying where anyone could trip over them and fall flat on his face. That might raise a laugh if it were someone else; but who's going to fall over them there?

**Mrs Paradock**  They'll come round presently.

**Mr Paradock**  All I can say is that I hope you're right.

**Mrs Paradock**  I wish that were all you could say. Except that you'd go on saying it all day long like a mentally deficient parakeet.

**Mr Paradock** A parakeet wouldn't necessarily have to be mentally deficient to keep saying the same thing over and over again. If that's all it's been taught, how can it say anything else? There's nothing mentally deficient about a parakeet acting according to its nature. It may be educationally subnormal, but that's another matter.

**Mrs Paradock** And when these two come round, which is more to the point, they're going to want some help in making us laugh. You'd better get down Bergson.

**Mr Paradock** They may hit us over the head with it when they come round.

*He goes to the bookshelf.*

**Mrs Paradock** It isn't very heavy. It's only a small book. I can see it from here – on the shelf. Not that one – that's right – now to the left, next to the blue one.

**Mr Paradock** (*taking down the book*) *Laughter.* Henri Bergson.

**Mrs Paradock** It's not big enough to do any damage even if they do hit you over the head with it. Now turn to page thirty-two and read out what it says.

**Mr Paradock** (*reads*) 'The fundamental law of life . . .' (*Gestures to the audience.*) Will they want to take notes?

**Mrs Paradock** They can read it for themselves when they get home.

**Mr Paradock** Oh. (*Reads.*) 'The fundamental law of life . . . is a complete negation of repetition! But I find that a certain movement of head or arm, a movement always the same, seems to return at regular intervals. If I notice it and it succeeds in diverting my attention, if I wait for it to occur and it occurs when I expect it, then involuntarily I laugh. Why? Because I now have before me a machine that works automatically. This is no longer life, it is automatism established in life and imitating it. It belongs to the comic.'

**Mrs Paradock** Good. And what does he say on page fifty-eight?

**Mr Paradock** He says, 'We laugh every time a person gives us the impression of being a thing.' You've marked it. But where does all this get us?

**Mrs Paradock** You'll see. These two are Bergson-trained.

**Mr Paradock** They'll be like that for hours yet.

*The two comedians begin to stir.*

**Mrs Paradock** Will they?

*The two comedians look around them as though coming out of a trance. Second Comedian leaves his chair and advances to the front of the stage. First Comedian follows.*

**Second Comedian** You could call this intellectual slapstick.

**First Comedian** We are, metaphysically, the Marx Brothers.

**Second Comedian** Presenting the custard-pie comedy of the abstract.

**First Comedian** Quintessentially.

**Second Comedian** And working to a blueprint.

**First Comedian** The fundamental law of life is a complete negation of repetition! But I find that a certain movement of head or arm, a movement always the same, seems to return at regular intervals.

*As he begins to recognise these words, Bro Paradock looks with some astonishment towards his wife, who*

*with a complacent half-smile sits down in one of the
vacated armchairs and takes up some knitting.*

If I notice it and it succeeds in diverting my attention, if
I wait for it to occur and it occurs when I expect it, then
involuntarily I laugh. Why? Because I now have before
me a machine that works automatically. This is no longer
life, it is automatism established in life and imitating it.
It belongs to the comic.

**Second Comedian** We laugh every time a person gives
the impression of being a thing.

*Bro Paradock comes forward to join them. The two
comedians adopt stage American accents.*

**Mr Paradock** Tell me something about this Bergson
method.

**First Comedian** You've never seen Bergson?

**Mr Paradock** Not that I can remember.

**First Comedian** He's never seen Bergson.

**Second Comedian** I thought everybody had seen Bergson
some time or another.

**First Comedian** You can't put it into words. You've just
got to see it.

**Mr Paradock** I understand he does it all by machinery.

**Second Comedian** He just comes on. That's all. He comes
on like he's a machine.

**Mrs Paradock** (*without looking up from her knitting*) It
sounds richly comic.

**Second Comedian** Remember that time he came on, the
way he was an electronic computer, and then had them
put straw in his hair?

**Mr Paradock** Can he do anything else? Can he do typewriters?

**First Comedian** He never has. What about it, Bug? Can Bergson do a typewriter?

**Mrs Paradock** He only wants to start selling you typewriter ribbons. It's a new sideline. Take no notice.

**Second Comedian** Typewriters don't make out too good comedy-wise, I guess.

**Mr Paradock** I want to be made up to look like an electronic computer. I want to raise a laugh.

**First Comedian** It's no good looking like an electronic computer. You've got to *be* an electronic computer.

**Mr Paradock** If Bergson can be an electronic computer for the laughs, so can I. What does an electronic computer do?

**First Comedian** Electronic computer? It's . . . well, it's electronic. What would you say was the difference, Bug?

**Second Comedian** What difference?

**First Comedian** It's like the human brain except it's electronic.

**Second Comedian** It's just the way they do things. They do it different. Why can't you stop asking questions?

**First Comedian** It thinks. Does calculations. Almost any calculation you like to think of as long as you feed the data into it first.

**Mr Paradock** Why don't we do calculations?

**Second Comedian** Hell.

**Mr Paradock** For the laughs. Multiply. Subtract. Like an adding machine.

**First Comedian**  But there are three of us.

**Mr Paradock**  A comptometer then. What does it matter? Tell me to do something. Go on. Feed me some data.

**First Comedian**  What sort of data?

**Mr Paradock**  Any sort. Just feed me. Tell me to add a hundred and ninety-three to six hundred and thirty-eight. Any damn thing.

**Second Comedian**  For crying out loud, a comptometer's got rows of black keys all over the top of it, for crissake, with numbers on!

**Mr Paradock**  Eight hundred and thirty-one!

**Second Comedian**  They gotta be pressed down!

**Mr Paradock**  That's the operator's job. Feed me some data.

**First Comedian**  And where's your lever mechanism?

**Mr Paradock**  Did Bergson say anything about a lever mechanism? The cube root of fifty thousand, six hundred and fifty-three . . .

**First Comedian**  (*to Second Comedian*) Unless he's electrically operated?

**Second Comedian**  It'd be more kinda realistic to have him bending forward like he was the right shape for a comptometer.

**Mr Paradock**  Thirty-seven!

**First Comedian**  I want him plugged in somewhere.

**Mr Paradock**  Three hundred and ninety-six thousand gallons of petrol at three and ninepence three-farthings a gallon allowing two per cent wastage . . .

*First Comedian passes his hands over Bro Paradock in
search of something, finds what he wants in his left
pocket and, putting his hand into the pocket, brings
out a three-pin plug attached to a length of flex. This
pays itself out from Bro Paradock's pocket.*

**Second Comedian** Bend him forward.

**First Comedian** Like this?

**Second Comedian** He ought to look more like he's got
keys.

**Mr Paradock** Seventy-five thousand five hundred and
ninety-four pounds fifteen shillings!

**Second Comedian** Get him plugged in. For God's sake
get him plugged in.

**Mr Paradock** Feed me some data.

**First Comedian** Play that flex out, Bug, will you? I'll plug
him in to the power point.

**Mr Paradock** Five times the cube root of pi r squared!
Give me a value for 'r'. In centimetres. Furlongs. Cubits.
Any damn thing.

   *First Comedian fits plug into socket.*

**Second Comedian** Switch it on.

**First Comedian** Oh. (*He does so.*) There. Now he's live.

   *Bro Paradock twitches and becomes tense. His face
   begins to work. Suddenly words burst out in a rapid
   torrent.*

**Mr Paradock** Paraparaparallelogrammatical. Eighteen
men on a dead man's chest at compound interest is not
what it's for for four in the morning when the square on
the hypotenuse is worth two in the circle two in the circle
two in the circle two in the circle . . .

**First Comedian** (*looks across, alarmed, at Second Comedian*) He's shorting!

**Second Comedian** The voltage wants fixing.

*Bro Paradock continues his monologue while First Comedian hurries to wrench out the plug.*

**Mr Paradock** Two in the circle two in the circle two in the circle two in the circle (*Plug comes out.*) two in the circle (*More calmly and increasingly slowly.*) at seven and six, and six and five, and five and four, and four and three, and three and two in the circle at six and five, and five and four, and four and three, and three and two in the circle at five and four, and four and three, and three and two in the circle at four and three, and three and two in the circle at three and two, and one, and nought.

*Bro Paradock unbends and mops his brow.*

I thought I was never going to get back. Who unplugged me?

**Second Comedian** You were shorting.

**Mr Paradock** You were pressing the wrong buttons. You can't do all that about pi r squared and compound interest on a comptometer. That's not what it's for. Of course I was shorting.

**First Comedian** You went haywire.

**Mr Paradock** I'm not surprised.

**Mrs Paradock** (*getting up*) I expect you'd all like some coffee after that.

**Second Comedian** Thank you, Mrs Paradock. We would.

**Mrs Paradock** You and Hamster will want it black, I expect, after your drunken orgy.

**First Comedian** Yes, please, Mrs Paradock. I think we finished up both those two bottles your husband opened for us.

**Second Comedian** I feel terrible.

**Mrs Paradock** I shan't be long. You'll feel better for a cup of coffee.

> *Middie Paradock goes out. Bro Paradock and the two comedians dispose themselves about the room as the lights fade out. A spotlight reveals a Technician in a white coat on, right. The living room remains in darkness while the Technician comes forward and addresses the audience.*

**Technician** I don't want to hold up the action for more than a minute or two, and in fact I have no intention of holding it up for as long as that. What we are doing here on the technical side is rather new and I have been asked to come out here on the stage and as quickly as I can without holding up the action longer than absolutely necessary to give you in a few words if I can just what it is we are trying to do on the technical side. You are not going to be approached in any way. Please be quite at ease on that score. This is not audience participation in any new and more exasperating form so do please relax and be quite natural. What we are doing is by way of being an experiment and it is an experiment we can only carry through successfully by at some stage in the production taking the audience – that is your good selves – into our confidence. We do this as much for our own sake as yours. We want you to be quite spontaneous. And that is why I am here now. To take you into our confidence. It is as I say a new technique and we do have of course a huge barrier to break down of prejudice if not outright hostility from those who are not fully conversant with what we are trying to do. Any opportunity of making our aims and methods more widely known is something we are always very glad to have extended to us and I on this occasion am very grateful to both you and those responsible for this production for being allowed to put you in the picture. This is a technique which can be used for any kind of stage production. Any production whatever that it is possible to mount on a stage where we have apparatus installed comes within our scope. But it is absolutely essential in every case for the audience to be as it were receptive to the need, if we are to be one hundred per cent effective, of as I say complete spontaneity. What we want, briefly, are your reactions. As you know, all of us react in the theatre. Laughter. Laughter is nothing more or less than a reaction. If we instinctively feel something to be funny, we laugh. In other words, we react. Now we have literally thousands of feet of microfilm on which we have recorded these reactions as and when they have occurred. These recordings we match up with recordings made on other reels of microfilm, recordings of whatever on the stage has acted as the stimulus for each reaction recorded. Let me illustrate. At one point in the performance, shall we say, a witticism comes into play. This witticism is picked up by our very sensitive detectors which also break it down into molecules. There is a reason for this. An author who makes use of our records gains a complete and accurate picture not only of the effectiveness of a given witticism as a whole, but is enabled to see, as though under a microscope, just which *part* of that witticism achieved maximum response. So you can see how essential it is that every member of the audience should react at optimum spontaneity from beginning to end of the performance. This ensures that at any given stage in the production the laughter response index which we pass on to the author and producer is as accurate and reliable as science can make it. Because that of course is what we are out to do. We hope in time with the co-operation of theatre managements and audiences all over the country to build up in microfilm a library which will embody the case histories in terms of audience reaction of a sufficiently large and representative number of productions of all kinds to do away with the need for inspired guesswork on the part of author or producer. Will this be funny? Or is one part of this likely to be more funny than some other, perhaps less funny, part? This is the kind of question the writer of comedy is always having to ask himself, and it's the kind of question we on the technical side feel we can supply a reliable answer to. And not only, of course, the writer of comedy. In tragedy too – where of course the response to be successful must always be a rather different response from that evoked by comedy – I hope I'm not holding up the action too much, but what we do feel we want to get established, and get more and more established, is the very real part we on the technical side can play. As I say, the writer of tragedy with his stock-in-trade of pity and terror is working just as much in the dark as his colleague of the comic muse. How much pity? Just what degree of terror? And so on. If there was audience resistance, what caused it? This is another question which, by classifying the laughter and tears we pick up, we can often answer for the bewildered author. If his audience according to our records are viscerotonic endomorphs, this may explain why his play, written shall we say, for cerebrotonic ectomorphs, fails to achieve saturation impact. And now I think I have held up the production long enough. I would only like to say in conclusion that we have the technique, and are only waiting for the green light to go right ahead and take the guesswork out of the inspiration for the ultimate benefit of you, the audience. Thank you for listening to me – and before I do finally finish, I would like to say how much we have been helped, very materially helped, by the way everyone responsible for this production down to the author himself has done everything possible to give us all the facilities we have asked for. And of course you, the audience, have given us what is our very life blood – your spontaneity. Thank you very much.

*He goes out. Lights come up in the living room. Bro Paradock and the two comedians are in various parts of the room, silent and blank. Middie Paradock enters with a tray of coffee cups and a jug of coffee.*

**Mrs Paradock** Did you think I was never coming?

**Mr Paradock** Ah, coffee.

**Mrs Paradock** Get the books out, Bro, will you?

**First Comedian** Don't get them out for me, Mrs Paradock. I never read.

**Mrs Paradock** Perhaps Bug would like a book with his coffee?

**Second Comedian** I do like a short book with coffee. Thank you, Mrs Paradock.

**Mrs Paradock** Now come on. Here's a place for you, Bug. Help Hamster to a chair, Bro. He's wearing his shoes crooked this week and I know they're hurting him. There are plenty of books at your elbow, Bug, and more in the bookcase if you want them. Hamster: now what are you reading?

**First Comedian** Nothing for me, thank you, Mrs Paradock. Just the coffee.

**Mrs Paradock** I can't get used to you not reading with your coffee.

**Second Comedian** He never has, Mrs Paradock.

**Mrs Paradock** Are we all settled? Come on, Bro. What are you going to have? Fiction, biography? I think I'll help myself to this textbook.

47

**Second Comedian** It looks rather nice.

**Mrs Paradock** Yes. Now we can all have a good read with our coffee.

**Mr Paradock** Shall I see what's on the wireless while we're reading?

**Mrs Paradock** That's right, Bro. See what's on. It ought to be the service.

**Mr Paradock** (*looking at his watch*) It'll be starting.

*Bro Paradock tunes in the wireless and all except First Comedian continue reading throughout. The prayers heard from the wireless are intoned in a voice of cultured Anglican fatuity, and the responses said in low-toned earnestness by a small chorus of voices, which is joined by First Comedian in an undertone.*

**Prayer** . . . weep at the elastic as it stretches:

**Mr Paradock** It's started.

**Response** And rejoice that it might have been otherwise.

**Prayer** Let us sing because round things roll:

**Response** And rejoice that it might have been otherwise.

**Prayer** Let us praise God for woodlice, and for buildings sixty-nine feet three inches high:

**Response** For Adam Smith's *Wealth of Nations* published in 1776:

**Prayer** For the fifth key from the left on the lower manual of the organ of the Church of the Ascension in the Piazza Vittorio Emanuele II in the town of Castelfidardo in Italy:

**Response** And for gnats.

**Prayer** How flat are our trays:

**Response**  Our sewers how underground and rat-infested altogether.

**Prayer**  As the roots of a tree strike downwards:

**Response**  So fire burns.

**Prayer**  As a river flows always towards its mouth:

**Response**  So is sugar sweet.

**Prayer**  Let us laugh therefore and be glad for the Balearic Islands:

**Response**  And sing with joy in the presence of dyspepsia.

**Prayer**  Let us give praise for those who compile dictionaries in large buildings, for the suitably clad men and women on our commons and in our hotels, for all those who in the fullness of time will go out to meet whatever fate awaits them, for the tall, the ham-fisted, the pompous and for all men everywhere and at all times.

**Response**  Amen.

**Prayer**  Let us give thanks for air hostesses and such as sit examinations, for the Bessemer process and for canticles, that all who live in France may be called Frenchmen and that nothing may be called useful that has no purpose.

**Response**  Amen.

**Prayer**  Let us talk and itch and swim and paint:

**Response**  Let us talk and itch and swim and paint.

**Prayer**  Let us make music, water, love and rabbit hutches:

**Response**  Let us make music, water, love and rabbit hutches.

**Prayer**  Let us be brave and punctual:

**Response**  And vituperative and good-looking.

**Prayer**  Let us laugh with those we tickle:

**Response**  Let us laugh with those we tickle.

**Prayer**  Let us weep with those we expose to tear gas:

**Response**  Let us weep with those we expose to tear gas.

**Prayer**  Let us throw back our heads and laugh at reality:

**Response**  Which is an illusion caused by mescaline deficiency.

**Prayer**  At sanity:

**Response**  Which is an illusion caused by alcohol deficiency.

**Prayer**  At knowledge: which is an illusion caused by certain biochemical changes in the human brain structure during the course of human evolution, which had it followed another course would have produced other biochemical changes in the human brain structure, by reason of which knowledge as we now experience it would have been beyond the reach of our wildest imaginings; and by reason of which, what is now beyond the reach of our wildest imaginings would have been familiar and commonplace. Let us laugh at these things. Let us laugh at thought:

**Response**  Which is a phenomenon like any other.

**Prayer**  At illusion:

**Response**  Which is an illusion, which is a phenomenon like any other.

**Prayer**  Let us love diversity:

**Response**  Because there is neither end nor purpose to it.

**Prayer**  Let us love simplicity:

**Response**  Because there is neither end nor purpose to it.

**Prayer** Let us think, and think we think, because leaves are green and because stones fall and because volcanoes erupt in a world where seas are salt.

**Response** Amen.

*The introductory bars of 'Sweet Polly Oliver' in an orchestrated version are heard from the wireless. First Comedian gets to his feet.*

**First Comedian** I think this is where we stand, isn't it?

*The Second Comedian, Bro and Middie Paradock have become aware of the music and begin to stand. Rather self-consciously they join in the hymn-like singing of 'Sweet Polly Oliver'. There is a momentary silence when the song ends, and then to neutralise their embarrassment they all try to be excessively normal.*

**Mrs Paradock** Now. Have we all had enough coffee?

**Second Comedian** It was splendid coffee, Mrs Paradock. You must show me how you make it.

**Mr Paradock** Middie's coffee is made by a secret process, Bug. Wild horses wouldn't drag it out of her.

**First Comedian** In that case we'll be making up ingenious excuses for coming round here every evening for coffee, Mrs Paradock.

**Mrs Paradock** You're both very welcome. Bro and I need some good comedians in the house to prevent us quarrelling all the time.

**Second Comedian** That's a bargain, then, Mrs Paradock. We supply the comedy, you supply the coffee.

**First Comedian** And if our comedy's as good as your coffee, Mrs Paradock, we shall all be more than satisfied.

**Mrs Paradock** Well, if no one wants any more coffee, I'll clear away the cups.

*Middie Paradock puts the cups and saucers onto the tray and takes this outside.*

**First Comedian** Did you know that a female cod can be the mother of eight million eggs?

**Mr Paradock** No.

**First Comedian** Eight million.

**Second Comedian** It's the apotheosis of irresponsibility.

**Mr Paradock** There'd be no counting them – not if there were eight million of them. Except on the fingers of eight hundred thousand pairs of hands.

**Second Comedian** Eight hundred thousand people to count the eggs of a single cod! It's ludicrous.

**Mr Paradock** And yet they call a female god a goddess.

**First Comedian** There's no accounting for it.

**Second Comedian** I'm not sure that I want to account for it. It's one of those things my imagination wilts at.

**Mr Paradock** I always thought you had a pretty strong imagination.

**First Comedian** He hasn't. Not for that sort of thing. He picked up an imaginary chair yesterday. I thought he was handling it remarkably easily, and when he sat down on it I knew why. It just crumpled up under him.

**Second Comedian** I should think Bro has got a strong imagination. Let's see you lift an imaginary chair, Bro, by the back legs.

**Mr Paradock** How?

**First Comedian** Get hold of it by the two back legs. Keep your arms straight out in front of you and see if you can bring it up to shoulder height. And hold it there.

**Mr Paradock** Where do I get the chair from?

**Second Comedian** Imagine it.

**Mr Paradock** Shall I?

**First Comedian** Go on.

> *Bro Paradock squats on his haunches, gets up and removes his jacket, squats again and adjusts his position before going through the motions of taking a grip on the back legs of a chair. His efforts to stand up with it are successful but strenuous. First Comedian picks up a chair which he places in Bro Paradock's outstretched hands. He holds this chair without effort.*

**Mr Paradock** That's extraordinary! I'd never have believed it.

**Second Comedian** You were letting your imagination run away with you.

**Mr Paradock** I'd never have believed it. The one I imagined I was lifting was twice as heavy as this one.

**First Comedian** You've just got a strong imagination. You're like me. I use it to develop my muscles.

**Second Comedian** Why don't you two have a contest of strength? We'll ask Mrs Paradock for a pair of scales when she comes in. See which of you can hang the heaviest weight on them.

**First Comedian** What do you say, Bro?

**Mr Paradock** I'm game if you are.

> *He goes to the door, opens it and puts his head out.*

Middie! Have we still got those scales?

> *Middie Paradock is heard off: 'As far as I know. What do you want them for?'*

I'll go and get them now.

*Bro Paradock goes out. Several seconds later Middie
Paradock comes in, followed by Bro Paradock with
the scales.*

**Mrs Paradock**  I hear you're going to have a trial of
strength between you.

**Second Comedian**  Not me, Mrs Paradock. It's these two.

**Mrs Paradock**  I'm surprised Bro's got a strong imagination
– I'd never have said so.

**Second Comedian**  Who's going to hold the scales? Shall
I hold them while you two get ready?

**Mr Paradock**  Isn't it going to be a bit heavy for you
when we both put weights on the end?

**First Comedian**  Don't worry about Bug. His imagination
isn't as strong as yours and mine, Bro. He won't register
more than a pound or two.

**Second Comedian**  I shall be all right. Now then. Here it is.
As soon as you're both ready.

**Mr Paradock** (*looking at First Comedian*) Shall we start?

**First Comedian**  Right. Here goes.

*Both pretend to be lifting massive weights, with
which they stagger towards the scales held by Second
Comedian. As they simultaneously hang their weights
on opposite arms of the scales, Second Comedian's
arm dips slightly as he takes the strain. The balance
remains horizontal.*

**Mrs Paradock**  Nothing in it. Fancy that.

**Mr Paradock** (*panting*) I don't know what was in it. It
weighed like cement.

**Mrs Paradock**  Bug seems to be managing it without
much difficulty.

**First Comedian** Better put it down now, Bug. It's putting too much strain on the scales. You'll have the joint starting.

**Second Comedian** (*lifting each load onto the floor in turn*) I don't know about cement. It feels like something a whole lot lighter than cement to me.

**Mrs Paradock** You must be stronger in the muscles, Bug.

**Second Comedian** It's his imagination, Mrs Paradock. It isn't equal to it.

**Mrs Paradock** Is that what it is?

*Silence.*

You forgot to ring up about the elephant, Bro.

**Mr Paradock** I thought you'd seen about it.

**Mrs Paradock** I have now. They're delivering it in the morning.

**Second Comedian** As for elephants, I must say we've started a fine lot of hares this evening. Don't you think so?

**Mr Paradock** March hares.

**First Comedian** We've started them all right. A whole lot of mad March hares streaking hell for leather across the open country.

**Second Comedian** And not one but will drop in its tracks before these worthy people pick up the scent.

*All turn to gaze thoughtfully at the audience.*

**Mrs Paradock** What a shame we can't give them a run for their money with tortoises.

*Curtain.*

# Act Two

*The living room. Bro Paradock, hands in pockets, is staring thoughtfully out through the window. Middie Paradock turns away from the window.*

**Mrs Paradock** It'll have to stay out.

*Bro Paradock turns slowly away and crosses the room.*

**Mr Paradock** What are the measurements?

**Mrs Paradock** You don't need measurements. A thing that size in a prefab.

**Mr Paradock** I thought we were living in a bungalow.

**Mrs Paradock** People will think we're trying to go one better than everybody else.

**Mr Paradock** It's only once a year for goodness' sake! You should have kept the measurements.

**Mrs Paradock** I should have gone for it myself instead of ringing. (*Turns to look out of the window.*) Look at it. Look at its great ears flapping about. Surely they know by now what size we always have.

**Mr Paradock** Perhaps they've sent us the wrong one.

**Mrs Paradock** It's big enough for a hotel. If you had a hotel or a private school or something you wouldn't need a thing that size.

**Mr Paradock** I suppose not.

**Mrs Paradock** And supposing it goes berserk in the night? I'm not getting up to it.

**Mr Paradock**  Why should it go berserk in the night any more than a smaller one?

**Mrs Paradock**  We'll have old Mrs Stencil round again if it does – threatening us with the RSPCA.

**Mr Paradock**  You should have been in when they came with it, then you could have queried the measurements.

**Mrs Paradock**  I can't think what we're going to call it. We can't call it Mr Trench again.

**Mr Paradock**  The only time we've not called it Mr Trench was three years ago when we had to make do with a giraffe.

**Mrs Paradock**  And look at the fuss we had before they'd take it in part exchange.

**Mr Paradock**  Of course they made a fuss. There was something wrong with it.

**Mrs Paradock**  (*looking through the window*) Imagine calling a clumsy great thing that size Mr Trench.

**Mr Paradock**  Why not?

**Mrs Paradock**  We can't go on year after year calling it Mr Trench.

**Mr Paradock**  You talk as if it were the same animal every time.

**Mrs Paradock**  You can hear the neighbours, can't you? They'll think we never launch out.

**Mr Paradock**  I know what you want to call it.

**Mrs Paradock**  It looks all the time as if we were hard up for a name to give the animal.

**Mr Paradock**  You want to call it Oedipus Rex, don't you?

**Mrs Paradock** It's better than Mr Trench year after year. At least it sounds as if we knew what was going on in the world.

**Mr Paradock** Oedipus Rex! (*He wags a finger archly through the window.*) Ah, ah! Only the *edible* blooms remember, Oedipus.

**Mrs Paradock** If you say it in that tone of voice of course it sounds ridiculous.

**Mr Paradock** (*in same tone*) Oedipus! Oedipus! You're letting that glass take *all* your weight!

**Mrs Paradock** Anything else would sound equally as ridiculous if you said it like that.

**Mr Paradock** It isn't Mr Trench we want a change from.

**Mrs Paradock** The only thing to do is ring up the Zoo. Tell them to come and collect it.

**Mr Paradock** And be without an elephant at all?

**Mrs Paradock** Tell them to come and collect it and the sooner the better. I'd rather not have one.

**Mr Paradock** I beg to differ.

**Mrs Paradock** We did without one the year we had a giraffe instead.

**Mr Paradock** I know we did without one the year we had a giraffe instead. And look at the trouble we had getting it changed. I don't want that all over again.

**Mrs Paradock** It's the RSPCA I'm worried about.

**Mr Paradock** They haven't been round yet. In any case you wouldn't get the Zoo at this time. They'll be closed.

**Mrs Paradock** I don't know why they couldn't send us what we asked for in the first place.

**Mr Paradock**  Is it any use trying to get hold of Eddie on the phone?

**Mrs Paradock**  Yes. Ring Eddie up. Or Nora. Nora'd be sure to know what to do. They used to keep pigeons and things. They had a room full of nothing else but different kinds of birds when they were all living at No. 89, and white mice and things.

**Mr Paradock**  It'll have to stay outside tonight.

**Mrs Paradock**  I'm not having it in the kitchen, if that's what you're leading up to.

**Mr Paradock**  If it starts straying all over the place during the night we shall have the RSPCA making a lot of difficulties.

**Mrs Paradock**  Not if we get it changed first thing. Get on to Nora.

**Mr Paradock**  If we're getting it changed first thing in the morning, where's the sense in thinking up a name like Oedipus Rex for it now?

**Mrs Paradock**  Because I'm not calling it Mr Trench six years running. You can if you like. I'm not.

**Mr Paradock**  I didn't want to call it Mr Trench the year it was a giraffe. That was your idea. It was your idea it would make a pleasant change to be giving the name to a giraffe instead of an elephant. Now you complain about calling it Mr Trench six years running.

**Mrs Paradock**  I think we'd be better off without it.

**Mr Paradock**  How would we?

**Mrs Paradock**  I do really. I think we'd be better off without. We've done nothing except bicker ever since they came with it.

**Mr Paradock** We weren't in when they came with it.

**Mrs Paradock** That's the whole point.

*Both relapse into silence. Bro Paradock takes up a paper. He looks up after an interval from his paper.*

**Mr Paradock** If we're going to change the name at all I can't see what you've got against Hodge for that matter.

**Mrs Paradock** Hodge is all right for a monkey.

**Mr Paradock** We'll go through some names and see what we can agree on. Hodge.

**Mrs Paradock** Hodge for a monkey. Gush for an elephant.

**Mr Paradock** Admiral Benbow.

**Mrs Paradock** Hiram B. Larkspur.

**Mr Paradock** Playboy.

**Mrs Paradock** Killed-with-kindness Corcoran.

**Mr Paradock** New-wine-into-old-bottles Backhouse.

**Mrs Paradock** 'Tis-pity-she's-a-whore Hignett.

**Mr Paradock** Lucifer.

**Mrs Paradock** Stonehenge.

**Mr Paradock** Haunch.

**Mr Paradock** *and* **Mrs Paradock** (*together*) Splinter.

**Mr Paradock** Thank God we can agree on something. Now I can ring Eddie.

**Mrs Paradock** Why ring up Eddie when you've got Nora who's had experience with animals? She could probably suggest something.

**Mr Paradock** (*dialling*) So you keep saying.

**Mrs Paradock**  Well?

**Mr Paradock**  Is that Mrs Mortice? . . . Oh . . . Will you? Thank you.

**Mrs Paradock**  You've decided to ring Nora, then.

**Mr Paradock** (*ignores her*)  Hello. Nora? . . . Yes, thank you, Nora. And how are you? . . . Oh? And what's that, Nora? . . . A what? . . . Hold on a moment, Nora . . . Yes . . . Yes . . . Hold on, Nora. Wait till I fetch Middie.

**Mrs Paradock**  Don't say they've got ours.

**Mr Paradock**  It's a snake. She says they ordered a snake and they've got one that's too short.

**Mrs Paradock**  Too short for what?

**Mr Paradock**  She says they're worried about the RSPCA.

**Mrs Paradock** (*takes up phone*)  Nora? . . . Yes, Bro was telling me. Isn't it maddening? . . . Yes . . . Yes – they've done exactly the same with us . . . No. About ten times too big. I don't know what the vanman was thinking about. A thing that size in a bungalow . . . Not indoors, no. We've got it out at the back . . . Yes. I think you're quite justified . . . No . . . No . . . Not till the morning, Nora. Bro thinks they'll be closed now anyway.

**Mr Paradock**  Why not ask her if she'd like to have Mr Trench and we'll take the snake off her.

**Mrs Paradock**  What? . . . No, I was talking to Bro, Nora. I think he's got some suggestion to make. I'll get him to tell you himself. (*Puts her hand over the mouthpiece.*) You talk to her. She's on about this snake of theirs.

**Mr Paradock**  What about it, Nora? If yours is on the short side it might do us very nicely . . . And you're welcome to Mr Trench . . . Yes. We don't need anything . . . No trouble at all, Nora . . . Yes? Well, that's better still . . . I'll come round with it, then . . . No . . . No, I'll remember . . . Yes, in about half an hour, then. Goodbye, Nora.

**Mrs Paradock**  Thank goodness we rang them up.

**Mr Paradock**  Did she say how short this snake was?

**Mrs Paradock**  She didn't give any measurements, if that's what you mean.

**Mr Paradock**  I thought perhaps you might have thought to ask her what the measurements were.

**Mrs Paradock**  Why didn't you ask her for the measurements yourself as far as that goes?

**Mr Paradock**  How was I to know whether you'd asked already?

**Mrs Paradock**  You heard me talking to her.

**Mr Paradock**  What have you done with my gumboots?

**Mrs Paradock**  What do you want gumboots for to go down the road a few doors with an elephant? Where are your other shoes?

**Mr Paradock**  These are my other shoes I've got on.

**Mrs Paradock**  And I should come straight back with Mr Trench. We don't want Mrs Stencil asking a lot of questions.

**Mr Paradock**  I notice you're all for calling it Mr Trench now you know it's a snake.

**Mrs Paradock**  What are you going to bring it back in? You can't have it on a lead like a canary.

**Mr Paradock**  In any case I thought we'd settled on Hodge for a name.

**Mrs Paradock**  Hodge for a jackal. Gush for an anaconda.

**Mr Paradock**  Admiral Benbow.

**Mrs Paradock**  Hiram B. Larkspur.

**Mr Paradock**  Playboy.

**Mrs Paradock**  We'll see how short it is first.

**Mr Paradock**  The only thing I've ever seen on a lead is a dog. I've never seen a canary on a lead.

**Mrs Paradock**  A dog on a lead, then.

**Mr Paradock**  I hate this job.

**Mrs Paradock**  You say that every year.

**Mr Paradock**  I've never had to do it before.

**Mrs Paradock**  You say it about other things.

**Mr Paradock**  If it comes to that, how do you know it *is* an anaconda?

**Mrs Paradock**  What else would it be? We shall have the RSPCA round while you stand there.

**Mr Paradock**  Good God!

*He goes out.*

**Mrs Paradock** (*slowly moving her head from side to side*) Admiral Benbow!

*Bro Paradock comes back into the room with his collar turned up. He turns it down and shakes rain from his jacket.*

You're not back already?

**Mr Paradock**  I'm not going in this rain.

**Mrs Paradock**  It's barely started.

**Mr Paradock**  I don't want to get mixed up in a lot of rain. I haven't got a hat for that sort of thing.

**Mrs Paradock**  You've got an eyeshield. What's wrong with that?

**Mr Paradock**  You gave it away.

**Mrs Paradock**  I don't mean that one. I mean the one you wear for tennis.

**Mr Paradock**  But that's to keep the sun out of my eyes.

**Mrs Paradock**  Can't you wear it back to front?

*Pause.*

**Mr Paradock**  What a coincidence! Uncle Fred! That's just what Uncle Fred used to do. When he was at sea. He used to wear an eyeshield back to front rather than be put to the expense of a sou'wester. It deflected the rainwater from his neck and the elastic band passed conveniently across his mouth like a horse's bit.

*A knock at the door. Middie Paradock goes to open it.*

**Mrs Paradock**  That would be too ingenious for you, of course.

*Nora is at the door.*

Nora! You're drenched! Come in.

**Nora**  I thought I'd better come over with this as soon as I saw it was raining. (*Fumbles in her handbag.*) I'm afraid I get terribly wet in these showers. I just haven't got that kind of a hat, I suppose. (*Takes out a pencil box.*) There. I said it was short, didn't I?

**Mrs Paradock**  Good gracious. Do I open it?

**Mr Paradock**  That's never an anaconda.

**Mrs Paradock**  Would Nora have brought it over if it had been? Perhaps I'll leave it in its loosebox. We don't want it eavesdropping.

*She puts the box, without opening it, on the mantelpiece.*

**Nora** (*looks into the mirror*) Goodness! My make-up.

**Mrs Paradock** Let me see. Oh, *no*. I think she's done very well, Bro, don't you? I admire you for coming out in it at all.

**Mr Paradock** It's a very good attempt, Nora. It takes a pretty good hat to manage a shower like that one. I didn't even try it. Not with my poor old hat.

**Nora** I don't know about that, Bro. I wouldn't mind having a hat like yours, anyway.

**Mrs Paradock** Hats aren't everything in this world. Far from it.

**Mr Paradock** I know they aren't everything.

**Nora** Some people seem to get by quite nicely without them. In fact I've often noticed it's the ones who haven't any hats at all who live the most satisfying lives in the long run.

**Mr Paradock** It isn't so much having the hats as knowing how to make the best use of them.

**Mrs Paradock** We can't all be blessed with hats.

**Mr Paradock** Look at Mrs Blackboy's husband and the showers he's got through in his time with that plastic shopping bag he carries round on his head.

**Nora** Or Bella for that matter. Bella's up half the night sometimes weatherproofing that old straw beehive she goes out in whenever she's got rain to cope with.

**Mrs Paradock** And a lot of those who are supposed to have such wonderful hats are going around half the time in other people's. I haven't got much time for them. They got them out of Christmas crackers more likely than not.

**Mr Paradock**  I don't like to see the time Bella spends on millinery. That sort of thing's all right if you've got millinery in your make-up. Otherwise leave it alone.

**Mrs Paradock**  Bro's not much of a one for millinery.

**Mr Paradock**  I don't get the time. I've got other things to do. Nora and I prefer to leave the showers to the ones with the hats, unless we're compelled to tackle them. And then we don't do too badly, eh, Nora?

**Mrs Paradock**  Nora's got plenty of hats, as you well know. Take no notice of him, Nora. He's only acting the fool. You shouldn't be so rude to people, Bro. It's lucky Nora knows you.

**Nora**  Oh, I've never made any pretensions to hats.

**Mrs Paradock**  You're too modest, Nora.

**Mr Paradock**  I've always known what I could do, and I've always known what I couldn't do. That's one of the reasons why I never became an air hostess.

**Nora**  Hasn't your Myrtle got a fine little hat on her head? I was noticing it only the other day.

**Mrs Paradock**  I don't know where she gets it from, then! Although I must say she didn't do too badly in her storm test last week. I will give Myrtle her due – she doesn't seem to worry much what weather she goes out in.

**Mr Paradock**  She gets it from Stan if she gets it from anybody. Or Uncle Fred.

**Nora**  Do you know what I think? It would never surprise me if Myrtle didn't turn out to be something of a storm-breaker before she's finished. She's got the hats for it.

**Mrs Paradock**  You're joking, Nora.

**Mr Paradock**  What about Uncle Fred, then? He did very nicely for himself with his eyeshield.

**Mrs Paradock** Exactly. It's Uncle Fred's eyeshield that got him where he was – you couldn't call him a natural storm-breaker. (*To Nora.*) Uncle Fred was Bro's uncle in the navy, Nora.

**Mr Paradock** He used to wear his eyeshield back to front so as to protect his neck from the rainwater.

**Mrs Paradock** Anybody would think he was a positive sou'wester man the way you talk.

**Mr Paradock** It wasn't that he didn't have a sou'wester, so much as that he could never get round to putting it on.

**Mrs Paradock** He never had one. You know perfectly well he used to borrow quite shamelessly from the other men whenever there was an important storm at sea and he couldn't get by with just his eyeshield.

**Nora** (*loudly*) Aha! Whose is the waste-paper basket? It looks rather interesting.

**Mrs Paradock** That's Mr Malden's. We lent him a couple of lampshades Myrtle has grown out of for his little boy; he said we were welcome to his waste-paper basket if we could make anything of it.

**Mr Paradock** It might be all right for Myrtle when she's older. It looks to me like one he had when he was at school.

**Nora** I rather think Myrtle's father has got his eye on it too, if I'm not too much mistaken.

**Mrs Paradock** He's tried it on for size. Didn't you, Bro? One night last week. But he won't be seen out in it.

**Mr Paradock** That sort of thing's all right for the summer.

**Nora** (*looks through the window*) Thank goodness it seems to have stopped raining, for the time being anyway.

**Mrs Paradock** Oh, splendid. Now you can take Mr Trench across to Nora's, Bro.

**Nora** I'll have to be going, then. I don't want to be out when you call, Bro.

**Mrs Paradock** That would never do, would it?

**Mr Paradock** It was lucky you got here when you did, Nora. I was just setting out. We might have missed each other.

**Nora** We might.

**Mrs Paradock** Not if you were both going the same way.

**Mr Paradock** We could hardly be going the same way when Nora was going in one direction and I was going in the other. How could we have been going the same way?

**Mrs Paradock** If you like, Nora, I'll hold Bro back for a few minutes. That'll give you time to get in and turn round before he comes knocking on the door.

*She holds him by the collar.*

**Nora** If you're sure it won't throw you out?

**Mrs Paradock** Of course it won't. It's no trouble keeping Bro back for twenty minutes or so. Especially when you're helping us out by taking the elephant off our hands.

**Nora** It'll be nice to get something with some size to it, believe me. I only hope you find you can make do with Bees' Wedding there. It was hopelessly short for us.

**Mrs Paradock** You've got the upstairs as well, of course, haven't you?

**Nora** And the cellar. We just can't do with anything smaller. We've managed in the past with a rhinoceros – we had that one the year before last, but it was barely large enough.

**Mrs Paradock** This one's a ridiculous size for us in this bungalow. We always like to have an elephant, of course, if we can, but we can't cope with one this size.

**Nora** What have you called it?

**Mrs Paradock** To tell you the truth, Nora, we haven't called it anything yet.

*Bro, still held firmly by the collar, has a barely perceptible spasm.*

We've hardly had time to get round to discussing names at all, and when we do we only seem to quarrel.

**Nora** Are you like that, too? We quarrel all the time over names.

**Mrs Paradock** Oh yes. We lose all control. Names and food. It's the only thing worth quarrelling about after all, isn't it?

**Nora** Every animal we've ever had all the time we've been here has been called 'Retreat from Moscow', whether it's been the one we ordered or not. We just can't agree on anything else, and so every year we end up calling it 'Retreat from Moscow'.

**Mrs Paradock** Never mind, Nora. Perhaps we'll be able to do without animals altogether one of these days.

**Nora** What a hope! But I mustn't keep you standing there with Bro. If you could just let him come on to us in about twenty minutes that'll give me time to open the gate at the back.

**Mrs Paradock** Goodbye, then, Nora. We'll be calling in on Sunday, remember.

**Nora** Make it as early as you can. Goodbye, Middie.

**Mrs Paradock** Goodbye.

*Nora goes out and Mrs Paradock closes the door, releasing Bro Paradock, who crosses the room, straightening his jacket.*

**Mr Paradock** What did you mean about that waste-paper basket? Telling her I tried it on.

**Mrs Paradock** Nora knew what I meant. It's just a private joke between us.

**Mr Paradock** I should think so.

**Mrs Paradock** I was surprised at you, if it comes to that. Starting her off on all that long rigmarole about hats. You know what always happens whenever we get on to that subject.

**Mr Paradock** I thought most of what she said was very sensible.

**Mrs Paradock** Bringing Uncle Fred into it like that.

**Mr Paradock** There was no need to disparage him in front of her and make everyone feel uncomfortable.

**Mrs Paradock** There was no need to bring Uncle Fred into it in the first place and then leave it to Nora to change the subject.

**Mr Paradock** Change what subject?

**Mrs Paradock** About the waste-paper basket. That was only to get you off Uncle Fred.

**Mr Paradock** I thought you said that was a private joke between the two of you.

**Mrs Paradock** So it was.

**Mr Paradock** I can't for the life of me in that case see how it was Nora changing the subject.

**Mrs Paradock** There's no point in raking over it all again now. I just get tired, that's all, of hats, hats, hats every time anyone calls. Especially Nora.

**Mr Paradock** It happened to have been raining.

**Mrs Paradock** I know it happened to have been raining.

**Mr Paradock** Then we can let the matter drop. Where are my gumboots?

**Mrs Paradock** You don't need gumboots to go down the road a few doors with an elephant. Where are your other shoes?

**Mr Paradock** These are my other shoes I've got on.

**Mrs Paradock** And I should come straight back with Mr Trench. We don't want Mrs Stencil asking a lot of questions.

**Mr Paradock** I notice you're all for calling it Mr Trench now you know it's going to somebody else.

**Mrs Paradock** We've been through all this before. For goodness' sake pull yourself together. We shall have the RSPCA round while you stand there.

**Mr Paradock** Perhaps we shall. Perhaps we shan't.

*He goes out. Middie Paradock sits down at the table with a glossy magazine.*

*The lights fade out in the living room and a half-light reveals two cleaners who, as they sweep perfunctorily, resting between bouts, are overheard in conversation.*

**First Cleaner** I didn't tell you about Len. He goes down the School of Building twice a week now, when he's not working.

**Second Cleaner** There's a lot of chances for them these days. More than what we had when we was their age.

**First Cleaner** He misses his darts now he can't go down The Grapes Tuesdays.

**Second Cleaner** Like Charlie with his wireless.

**First Cleaner** He won the darts championship the other week, his team.

**Second Cleaner** He misses his wireless. He always goes to the cupboard first thing when he gets in off leave. 'Mum,' he says, 'what you done with the soldering iron?' He come home Sunday.

**First Cleaner** Len'll have to go soon.

**Second Cleaner** Goes back Sunday night. He's put in for apprentice fitter but he don't know if he'll hear anything.

**First Cleaner** He was talking about getting deferred, but I said to him, 'If you get deferred you'll only have it hanging over you.'

**Second Cleaner** Charlie's made one or two pals where he is. They get a bit fed up with all the routine.

**First Cleaner** They all do. It's only natural.

**Second Cleaner** Everything has to be done to orders and that.

**First Cleaner** What Len's hoping is he'll get in the Raf. That's what he's started down at the School of Building for, so he can say he's done something.

**Second Cleaner** How's Gran?

**First Cleaner** Up and down. She can't get about like she used.

**Second Cleaner** You heard about Mrs Jarvis?

**First Cleaner** Flo told me.

**Second Cleaner** She'll have his pension, but it's not the same.

**First Cleaner** Mr Braithwaite went round from the chapel. Spoke very nice. Said to keep praying and that. 'The Lord will provide, Mrs Jarvis,' he said.

**Second Cleaner** He can't give her what Jarvis could.

**First Cleaner** Shh! You'll have them dirty old men out the back listening.

**Second Cleaner** It's true, isn't it? I reckon she'll miss him that way unless she can find somebody else.

**First Cleaner** I didn't tell you what old Mrs Croskett told me when she was round Mrs Jarvis's.

**Second Cleaner** I didn't know she'd been round there.

**First Cleaner** She's been round there twice. So's Mrs Blench. They both said you wouldn't have thought there was nothing wrong with him to see him eat the night before, and then next day he come over funny at work.

**Second Cleaner** Remember last winter when he was down with the gastric and nobody couldn't say what it was?

**First Cleaner** I'll tell you when I started putting two and two together a bit – you know he had that great thick overcoat? The one he had for when he was going anywhere? She's got that out, so Mrs Croskett was saying, and she's got all the seams unpicked and she's going to put a bit of felt lining under it after she's cut it up, and make mats out of it.

**Second Cleaner** Isn't that Else over there, coming across?

*Middie Paradock appears as though relaxing off the set.*

**First Cleaner** I didn't know you'd decided to have another go at the stage, Else.

**Mrs Paradock** It's only while Fred's on night work. I thought I'd keep my hand in. I never expected to see you here, though.

**Second Cleaner** You used to be all for gay parts.

**Mrs Paradock** This one's not so bad. It makes a change.

**Second Cleaner** I don't know how you can remember your lines – it sounds like a lot of rigmarole to me.

**First Cleaner** Everything's that trend nowadays.

**Mrs Paradock** It's all right if you don't think about it. A lot of it's supposed to be symbolic, but you get used to it.

**Second Cleaner** I don't know, I'm sure.

**First Cleaner** How's Fred, Else?

**Mrs Paradock** Fred's fine, thanks, Mrs Gride. We're going down the tabernacle Sundays now. There's a new man there. Mr Brice. Took Mr Jabez' place Christmas. He gets a good crowd Sunday evenings.

**Second Cleaner** That's nice.

**Mrs Paradock** Fred's very taken with him. We're going to go to the midweek service when he's on early turn if I can get away.

**First Cleaner** Wasn't Edie telling us about a Mr Brice?

**Mrs Paradock** We saw Edie there Sunday. He was ever so good on 'What the Church Means to Me'. He's going through all different aspects: at home, you know, and at work and that. Next week it's 'What the Church Means to Me on Holiday'. He gets a lot going up the mercy seat every Sunday. Fred was on at me to go up but I had my old coat on.

**Second Cleaner**  You feel everybody's looking at you, like when Mrs Leakey stood up and give testimony that time we had the women's meeting in the Temperance Hall.

**First Cleaner**  The Temperance Hall was when we went down Eastbourne with the outing.

**Second Cleaner**  That's right. Surely you remember Mrs Leakey? Kep' on all the way back in the coach about she's saved, she's saved all the time.

**Mrs Paradock**  It's the thanksgiving Sunday week. Why don't you and Mrs Gride come over?

**Second Cleaner**  We'll see what the weather does, Else dear. It's a long way with my legs – the journey knocks me over.

**First Cleaner**  (*nodding towards the set*) You look as if you're wanted, Else.

**Mrs Paradock**  (*waves her hand*) It's only Sam, but I suppose I'd better go. Must be time. I expect you'll both be gone by the time I'm finished so I'll say goodbye. Goodbye, Mrs Gride. Remember me to Len. Goodbye, Mrs Quiller.

*She goes back to the set, which remains in darkness. The rest of the stage remains dimly lit. A spotlight is turned on to the cleaners.*

**First Cleaner**  Goodness! They've turned the lights on us!

**Second Cleaner**  That'll be Bert's idea of a joke.

*They gather up buckets and mops and hustle each other out.*

They've properly caught us with our trousers down.

**First Cleaner**  Shh! You'll have us locked up!

75

*Blackout. Lights in the set go up. Middie Paradock is sitting at the table as before, reading a glossy magazine. She puts it away, and begins a game of patience.*

**Mrs Paradock** (*without looking up*) Come in.

*She continues in thought, places two more cards on the table, looks towards the door and repeats 'Come in.' When nothing happens, she impatiently puts down the cards and goes to the door. As she opens it to find no one there, the two comedians enter by the door behind her, sit at the table and continue the game of patience. She turns away from the door, closing it, and speaks half to herself, and half to the two at the table, whose presence she takes for granted.*

I made sure that was somebody at the door.

*She stands for a moment watching the game.*

Don't you two ever get tired of patience?

**First Comedian** We've been drinking again, Mrs Paradock.

**Mrs Paradock** So you've taken my advice, have you?

**Second Comedian** We feel a whole lot tipsier for it.

**Mrs Paradock** Isn't that what I told you? You never listen to me.

**Second Comedian** It was that delicious ambrosia you gave us when we were here last week, Mrs Paradock. That was what put us on to drinking.

**Mrs Paradock** It's a very stimulating drink. Bro and I keep coming back to it, and the surprising thing is we're always finding something fresh to make us drunk in it. I'm glad you both like it.

**First Comedian** We've gone on to other things since, of course. What was it we were drinking last weekend? Bug said he couldn't remember when a drink left him so well oiled.

**Second Comedian** Raven's Blood – but I thought the name was the weakest part of it. What I enjoyed was the glass in the middle of the bottle. I spent a long time over that – just savouring it.

**Mrs Paradock** Bro's in the middle of a good bottle now. I'll get him to pour you out drops of it when he comes in.

**First Comedian** Where is Bro, Mrs Paradock?

**Mrs Paradock** He's out with an elephant, but he should be back. We had one delivered that was too big for what we want, so we've done a sort of switch with Mrs Mortice. She's left us this snake – (*Takes down pencil box from shelf.*) – and Bro's taking our elephant round to her.

*She opens the box.*

**First Comedian** It looks hardly long enough for a snake.

**Mrs Paradock** You can have them lengthened, but we shan't bother.

**Second Comedian** I think snakes are too long for what you generally want them for. People just like to go one better than everybody else.

**Mrs Paradock** (*glances out through the window*) Here's Bro now.

*She goes to open the door.*

You've been a long time.

*Bro Paradock comes in, swaying a little, but otherwise normal in his manner.*

**Mr Paradock** I've been in the pub on my way back. Hello, Bug. Hello, Hamster, old boy. I got stuck into a bottle in the pub and I couldn't tear myself away. I'm trying to remember what it was called. You two would enjoy it.

**Mrs Paradock**  You look as if you've been having a good old drink, doesn't he, Bug? His eyes are all bloodshot . . .

**Second Comedian**  I think Mrs Paradock is the only one of us who –

*Pause.*

**Mrs Paradock**  Finish what you were going to say, Bug.

**Second Comedian**  No, I'd rather leave it at that, Mrs Paradock.

**Mr Paradock**  You were in the middle of a sentence, for God's sake!

**First Comedian**  He does that sometimes. He often leaves a sentence unfinished. It's more effective. It's like a sawn-off shotgun.

**Mrs Paradock**  (*grimacing*) I don't like the sound of that remark.

**Mr Paradock**  What's wrong with it?

**Mrs Paradock**  I don't like the sound of it. It sounds as if it's on the turn to me.

**Mr Paradock**  It would have turned before now if it was going to turn.

**Second Comedian**  It's only the sound of it, Mrs Paradock.

**Mrs Paradock**  That remark will be paradoxical tomorrow morning when it comes out of the subconscious. You can't tell me anything about paradoxes.

**First Comedian**  Reminds me of an old stage designer who after a lifetime of faking stage props to look genuine had to admit defeat for the first time when he had to fake something to look bogus.

**Second Comedian** Talking about paradoxes, what about the platoon sergeant who sent his men into a wood to take cover and when they got there, said: 'You can take it easy, now, lads. We're out of the wood!'

**Mrs Paradock** You men. You're all as bad as one another, with your horrible paradoxes.

**Mr Paradock** Let's put the case of someone forgetting his lines on the stage at the exact point where he's supposed in the play to pretend to have forgotten them.

**First Comedian** I don't think I follow. You're a bit too drunk for me.

**Mr Paradock** He has to give the illusion that he's forgotten his lines. As part of the play. All right?

**First Comedian** Yes. I follow that.

**Mr Paradock** Now. At the precise moment when he's supposed to give the illusion of having forgotten his lines, he quite forgets what it is he has to do. His mind goes blank. So what happens? There's a pause. The pause prolongs itself. But sooner or later he remembers what it is he ought to have been doing. He ought to have been giving the impression of having been at a loss for words. There's nothing he can do about it now. The audience will have to make do with the reality instead of the illusion – which would probably have been much better. They might well have had to do without both. He might well have forgotten not only that he was supposed to stumble for words, but that there was anything he was supposed to do at all. In that case he'd have gone straight on – word perfect.

**Mr Paradock** Thus – the illusion of having remembered may be sustained only by forgetting, and the illusion of having forgotten only by remembering.

**Mrs Paradock** I've only one thing against these paradoxes. They're like puns – they're just plays on words when you analyse them. I don't mind good, solid, practical puns. I don't mind a pun in real life that means something. In fact I like to see somebody using his boot as a hammer, for instance. That's a practical pun.

**Mr Paradock** That can be carried too far as well.

**Second Comedian** Hamster's brother-in-law's a great practical punster. I remember the time he threw a vase at a cat. It was a beauty. It did as much damage as a genuine missile and he used it to put flowers in afterwards.

*A knock. Middie Paradock goes out.*

**Mr Paradock** It's a pity you can't use an umbrella stand in the breech of a fifteen-inch naval gun. If you could I should feel a whole lot happier about using a shell-case as a doorstop.

**First Comedian** That's life, Bro. It's no use looking for an editorial in a tablecloth simply because you eat your meals off a newspaper.

*Middie Paradock comes in with an opened telegram, which she is reading.*

**Mrs Paradock** It's Don and that motor scooter again. I shall be glad when we see the last of that craze.

**Mr Paradock** What's he up to this time?

**Mrs Paradock** Read it. (*Hands the telegram to Bro. To the others.*) He's been parking his motor scooter on that piece of waste ground again behind Rachmaninov's Second Piano Concerto.

**Mr Paradock** Who does that belong to?

**Mrs Paradock** It doesn't belong to anybody. It's just a piece of waste ground.

**Mr Paradock** Then they can't stop him parking his motor scooter on it if it doesn't belong to anyone.

**Second Comedian** What does the telegram say, Mrs Paradock?

**Mr Paradock** (*he is still holding the telegram*) 'Arriving twelve-ten Euston send sandwiches.'

*He hands the telegram to Second Comedian.*

**First Comedian** I shouldn't let that upset you, Mrs Paradock. It doesn't mean what it says.

**Mr Paradock** The last time we had a telegram like this it was worded very differently.

**First Comedian** I should just say nothing about the motor scooter. Say nothing to him about it. When he's gone to bed perhaps you can find a salesman to sell it to.

**Mrs Paradock** I doubt it. He bought it from a buyer.

**Second Comedian** You can set your minds at rest about the telegram. It's in code.

**Mrs Paradock** Thank heaven for that.

**Mr Paradock** How can you tell it's in code?

**Second Comedian** There's no way of telling, I'm afraid. It either is or it isn't. This one is.

**First Comedian** I thought it was from the beginning. The moment Mrs Paradock came in with it. You can always tell with a telegram. As Bug says, it's either in code or it isn't.

*The door opens. Don, a smartly dressed woman in her twenties, comes in.*

**Second Comedian** Here's Don now.

**Mrs Paradock** Don! Why, you've changed your sex!

**Don**  Didn't you get my telegram?

**Mr Paradock**  We got it all right, but it was in code.

**Don**  It shouldn't have been. I asked them to decode it before they sent it off.

**Mrs Paradock**  Never mind. I always wanted a girl.

**Mr Paradock**  That's the first I knew of it.

**First Comedian**  Now perhaps we can have that conversation we promised ourselves about the conversation we had at the Wordsworths'.

**Mrs Paradock**  So we can. I've been waiting to hear all about it. I expect Don there's feeling like a good long conversation after travelling up to Euston since four o'clock this morning. What were the trains like this time, Don?

**Don**  Don't talk about them, Mother. One long compartment after another.

**Mr Paradock**  Well, let's start this conversation. How was it we broke the ice at the Wordsworths'? What was it we began with? A noun clause each, wasn't it?

**Don**  That's right. We were all given a noun clause each – in apposition – and then we had to go round asking everyone in turn for the noun it was in apposition to, till we found the right one.

**Mrs Paradock**  I suppose John was as much in demand as ever with his adverbial clauses?

**Don**  Oh, John! John's got a thing about his adverbial clauses.

**First Comedian**  He can be a bit childish about them, too, at times. Over those subordinating conjunctions, for instance, that he said were prepositions.

**Don** That was Margaret. What actually happened was that he asked for subordinating conjunctions and she handed him these prepositions thinking they were adverbs or something.

**Second Comedian** And then to make matters worse she said, 'Will these do? I can never tell the difference myself.'

**First Comedian** 'I can never tell the difference'! What a thing to say to John of all people.

**Don** You know that little spot of high colour he gets on the side of his forehead whenever he's annoyed at anything . . .

**First Comedian** Annoyed! It was all he could do to be civil to her.

*Bro Paradock stands apart from the others, staring tight-lipped into the distance.*

**Second Comedian** Tell them about Joe, Hamster.

**First Comedian** Joe?

**Don** And the figures of speech.

**First Comedian** Oh. 'Give me good plain syntax,' you mean? I don't think he'd met half the figures of speech before.

**Second Comedian** I happened to look up when someone put that synecdoche in front of him. 'What's this?' he said. 'Metonymy?'

**First Comedian** Metonymy!

**Don** What about Mrs Kapellmeister, then? Falling over herself almost for a transferred epithet every time one appeared. I suppose she was afraid someone else might get to them first.

**Mrs Paradock** Looking at her husband sometimes, I'm surprised to hear she didn't go for oxymoron. I've never seen anyone who looks more like the original sustained metaphor than he does.

**Don** He's certainly at the opposite end of the pole from her.

**Mrs Paradock** It's only zeugma that keeps them together.

*She goes across to where Bro Paradock is still morosely standing, while the others continue talking amongst themselves.*

What's the matter with you? Moping over here on your own?

**Mr Paradock** There's nothing the matter with me at all.

**Mrs Paradock** Why can't you join in the conversation then? Standing here saying nothing.

**Mr Paradock** I'm standing here saying nothing because I can't think of anything to say. I should have thought that was obvious.

**Mrs Paradock** Can't think of anything to say! Surely you could define 'consanguinity' or something.

**Mr Paradock** What chance have I had to define 'consanguinity'?

**Mrs Paradock** You've had just as much chance as anybody else. For goodness' sake, come and join in the conversation even if it's only to contradict somebody.

*Reluctantly, and with the look of a martyr, Mr Paradock goes towards the others.*

**Mr Paradock** My wife wants me to take part in the conversation.

**Second Comedian** We were just saying what a good party it was, by and large.

**Don** It would have been if that girl with co-ordinate clause written all over her face hadn't tried to monopolise Max all evening.

**First Comedian** At least we were spared Charles this time with his endless paronomasia.

**Don** I'd rather have Charles than that one with the dreary onomatopoeia who was doing farmyard imitations with it every five minutes.

**First Comedian** Oh no. Not farmyard imitations?

**Don** He was. I thought he was never going to stop, and then when Margaret asked him if he ever added to his repertoire and he did half-a-dozen new ones I could have killed her. It was only the thought of her adverbial clauses of concession that stopped me, I think.

**Second Comedian** I can't say they impressed me all that much. They've nothing like the sheer architectonic qualities, for instance, of successive adjectival clauses one on top of another in the hands of a master.

**Mr Paradock** Architectonic archbishops! I could give you some adjectival clauses that would scorch the seat off your pants to listen to them. (*Loudly.*) This is the soldier that loved the wife that poisoned the hangman that hanged the murderer that shot the assassin that stabbed the king that won the war that killed the soldier that loved the wife that poisoned the hangman that hanged the murderer that shot the assassin that stabbed the king that won the war that killed the soldier that loved the wife that . . .

**Mrs Paradock** For goodness' sake pull yourself together! It's in bad taste. Can't you forget you're an undertaker once in a while?

**Second Comedian** I never knew Bro was an undertaker.

**First Comedian** Neither did I. I'd noticed he was always rather partial to death. Now I see why.

**Mrs Paradock** It's his life.

**Mr Paradock** It's just that I see things from an undertaker's point of view.

**Mrs Paradock** There's no need to make everyone feel uncomfortable just because you can't arrive at a definition of 'consanguinity'. He's set his mind on defining 'consanguinity' and there's no shifting him. Everything else has to take second place when he's in this mood.

**Mr Paradock** All I want is a chance to define *something*. It doesn't have to be 'consanguinity'. That was your suggestion. It isn't as if I often get the time for defining things.

**Mrs Paradock** Or the inclination.

**First Comedian** I think we'd better be off, Bug. Remember you're expecting a phone call at nine o'clock.

**Second Comedian** She rang this morning.

   *First Comedian nudges him.*

She'll be ringing me again, though, at nine o'clock. I wasn't in this morning. No one answered the phone.

**First Comedian** Goodbye, Mrs Paradock.

**Mrs Paradock** You're not going?

**First Comedian** Bug's got a phone call he's expecting and I ought to be getting back to my filing.

**Mrs Paradock** (*out of Bro's hearing*) He'll be all right tomorrow.

**Second Comedian** We'll look in, Mrs Paradock, and see how he is.

**Don** Don't you worry about Father. We'll get him to bed with a hot-water bottle.

*They go out.*

**Second Comedian** Goodbye, Mrs Paradock. Goodbye, Bro.

**First Comedian** Are you coming out with us, Don?

**Don** I've got to go down the road a little way.

**First Comedian** Goodbye, Bro. Goodbye, Mrs Paradock.

**Mrs Paradock** Look after yourselves.

*Middie Paradock closes the door and turns back to Bro.*

A fine exhibition you made of yourself.

**Mr Paradock** Where's Don?

**Mrs Paradock** Gone where you can't harm her any more with your bitter words.

**Mr Paradock** I think I'll have a turn in the garden.

**Mrs Paradock** We haven't got a garden. You know that as well as I do.

**Mr Paradock** I understood we had. It's in the deeds.

**Mrs Paradock** Is it?

**Mr Paradock** I wouldn't have bought the house otherwise.

**Mrs Paradock** House? This is a bungalow.

**Mr Paradock** I wouldn't have bought it without looking pretty closely at the deeds to see if there was any mention of a garden.

**Mrs Paradock** If you can find a garden in the deeds of this place you're welcome to take a turn in it.

*There is a pause while Bro ponders this.*

I should get up to bed if I were you.

**Mr Paradock** *Up* to bed? I thought we were living in a bungalow?

**Mrs Paradock** Look, Bro. I'm trying to help you. You're being very difficult and perverse and I'm trying very hard to be reasonable with you and understand you. Don't forget I'm just as drunk as you are underneath and I'm trying to fight it for both of us. You don't make it very easy for me, Bro.

**Mr Paradock** I didn't know you were drunk too. I thought it was just me.

**Mrs Paradock** You never do think it's ever possible for me to feel a bit blotto from time to time, Bro. You think you're the only one who takes a pull at the bottle occasionally.

**Mr Paradock** I sometimes envy the man in the street who's never learned to drink for himself at all.

**Mrs Paradock** It's no good getting cynical, Bro.

**Mr Paradock** I do get cynical sometimes. The average man seems to be quite content to let the rest of us do all his drinking for him.

**Mrs Paradock** That's true, Bro, but although he's spared a lot of the hangovers, don't forget that he misses the intoxication too.

**Mr Paradock** Perhaps you're right, Middie, my dear.

**Mrs Paradock** And now we must get out of here, Bro, because the producer wants it for his critics' meeting or something in a few minutes. So up you get.

*She helps him out. Lights fade out.*

*Author's mouthpiece appears to right of set.*

**Author** It seemed the only way. I think we have all been trying as hard as can reasonably be expected not to show our exasperation – I certainly have – because we do all like, naturally, to feel we've been provided with a meaning; something we can carry round with us like an umbrella for a few days. We all feel rather lost without a meaning to seize hold of; rather like a snake charmer in front of a boa constrictor and no flute. Or whatever they use. And in this search for a meaning we have some very good allies in the critics. They know a great deal about these things. They are trained to find meanings, and even if there are no meanings to be found they rarely come unprovided with spare meanings which with a little wire and string can often be fastened quite securely. So it is to the critics that for all our sakes I have decided to turn. We've got to turn somewhere. And what help I could have given you would have been worse than useless. I lay claim to no special vision and my own notions as to what it is I have in mind here may well fall pitifully short of your own far better notions. No. I am the dwarf in the circus – I give what scope I can to such deficiencies as I have. Beyond that, it is to these public servants of ours who guide us all to destinations (which even though they may not always amount to very much as destinations are nevertheless the best destinations we have), it is to the critics that we must commit ourselves. But for them we would be hard put to it to arrive anywhere at all. And it's the arriving somewhere which gives us the illusion that the journey has been worthwhile. No such illusion is likely to trouble any of us here, but perhaps we need not go home altogether empty-handed for all that – because here they are. Here is the first of the critics. This is, I need hardly tell you, a very welcome sight. I think we are shortly going to be led out of the wilderness. It's Mustard Short, you've probably recognised him, who has just taken his seat.

*The critics as they arrive sit down round the table in the living room. Mustard Short is the first to arrive, but is closely followed by Denzil Pepper, who takes a chair opposite him. When Miss Salt and Mrs Vinegar come in together they occupy the remaining seats, leaving a seat vacant at the head of the table for the Chairman.*

It was Mustard Short, as you know, who last year – or was it earlier than that, in some previous incarnation perhaps? – who drew attention to some faults of structure in *Tristram Shandy*. And here is Denzil Pepper, carrying his high standards invisibly in brown paper, manoeuvring them clear of the light fittings and as ready devastatingly to unwrap them here as anywhere else. 'If this weren't in a bucket,' he roars, getting a lump of soap and plunging his hands into a bucket of sulphuric acid, 'if this weren't in a bucket, I should never have guessed it was meant to be water!' He's the boy. He's the one, if anybody can, who'll unmask the shadow. In a bloody froth of fulmination, too, unless he happens to have taken a sedative. Mrs Vinegar there – she's the woman in the black suit who has just sat down on the left of Mustard Short – looks, I must say, disconcertingly the worse for tedium. Miss Salt, on the other hand, is clearly ready to begin digging with indefatigable trowel among whatever unfruitful clods of dramatic earth she finds at her dedicated feet, and may, for all we can tell, come upon something which will surprise us all. And now let us alert the coastguards of our minds, for the Chairman has arrived. We must try now to assume receptive postures, and be ready to give asylum to such thoughts as are shortly to come among us.

*Lights, except in the living room, fade.*

**Chairman** (*standing*) Shall we ask a blessing?

*All stand.*

For what we are now about to bestow may we be made truly worthy.

**Salt**  I protest!

**Pepper**  I deplore!

**Mustard**  I condemn!

**Mrs Vinegar**  I denounce!

**Miss Salt**  I wish to go on record as having cringed.

**Pepper**  I wish to go on record as having writhed.

**Mustard**  I wish to go on record as having squirmed.

**Mrs Vinegar**  I wish to go on record as having suffered agony.

**Miss Salt**  I hail!

**Pepper**  I salute!

**Mustard**  I predict!

**Mrs Vinegar**  I acclaim!

**All**  (*loudly and in unison*) I wish to go on record! I wish to go on record! I wish to go on record!

   *They sit.*

**Chairman**  We'll start at once with a discussion of the performance we have all been watching for the last hour or so, and we'll begin by deciding, if we can, what it is we have been present at, before going on to a consideration of its merits. Is this piece the bold experiment some people hold it to be? Is it a shameless plagiarism from the pen of a true primitive of the theatre – as someone has said – or is it neither of these things? Denzil Pepper – what do you make of this?

**Pepper**  This is a hotchpotch. I think that emerges quite clearly. The thing has been thrown together – a veritable ragbag of last year's damp fireworks, if a mixed metaphor is in order.

**Miss Salt** Yes. I suppose it *is* what we must call a hotch-potch. I do think, though – accepting Denzil Pepper's definition – I do think, and this is the point I feel we ought to make, it is, surely, isn't it, an *inspired* hotchpotch?

**Pepper** A hotchpotch de luxe. Only the finest ingredients. A theatrical haggis.

**Chairman** Isn't this what our ancestors would have delighted in calling a gallimaufry?

*Pause.*

**Mustard** 'They have made our English tongue a gallimaufry or hodgepodge of all other speeches.' Yes. Spenser in the letter to Gabriel Harvey at the beginning of *The Shepherd's Calendar*. Yes. I'm not sure that I don't prefer the word 'gallimaufry' to Denzil Pepper's 'hodgepodge'.

**Pepper** Hotchpotch. No. I stick, quite unrepentantly, to my own word.

**Miss Salt** I'm wondering whether what Spenser was saying there was not referring to the language itself rather than to what was said in it? Words and phrases borrowed from other languages and so on? I think perhaps – and I say this under correction: I know Mustard Short is more familiar than I am *about* the attitude to this kind of thing in James Joyce – isn't this . . . haven't we got here an actual *repudiation* on the Joycean model *of* orderliness in a way the writers Spenser was attacking had not?

**Pepper** I'm not at all happy about letting him get away with it on his own terms like that. After all, what happens when a boxer gets knocked out in the ring? He's lost the fight. It's as simple as that. He's lost the fight, and it makes no difference that his manager or someone announces through the loudspeaker afterwards that lying flat on his back was a deliberate repudiation of the vertical.

**Mrs Vinegar** I couldn't agree more.

**Chairman** Mrs Vinegar.

**Mrs Vinegar** I was bored with this play. Or whatever it is. I was bored almost from the rise of the curtain with the characters – or is 'characters' too strong a word ? – and I was even more bored by the situations they were put into.

**Mustard** And the acting? Were you bored with the acting? I thought the cast carried it off for him exceptionally well.

**Pepper** A splendid cast.

**Mustard** Quite exceptionally well.

**Miss Salt** It was in fact an actors' play.

**Mustard** An actors' play and of course in a way a producer's play.

**Chairman** How would Mrs Vinegar feel about calling this an actors' play?

**Mrs Vinegar** No. No, I thought the acting was extremely good. The production I'm less sure about, but it was quite sound. As for this being an actors' play or a producer's play, whatever that may mean, I think fifth-rate play is the only sound designation for it. No amount of talent on the stage can make a fifth-rate play into a third-rate one, although it was quite obvious that that was what they were aiming at.

**Chairman** Mustard Short. Were you bored by this play?

**Mustard** Bored, no. Exasperated at times, yes. I did, I think, suppress a mild yawn twice, but I smiled occasionally, wondered what was coming next, got annoyed and irritated fairly frequently – in fact reacted much as one does in the theatre, except for experiencing tension. There was no tension and no tears. That I think was a pity because with so much else there it would have been nice for the sake of completeness to have had those as well.

**Mrs Vinegar** May I ask Mustard why, if he felt a genuine desire to yawn, he suppressed it?

**Mustard** Politeness, I suppose – it's a vice we're all prone to in the theatre, where we could do with a lot less of it.

**Miss Salt** If only to keep Aunt Edna in Surbiton.

**Mrs Vinegar** The way to keep Aunt Edna or anybody else in Surbiton is to go on putting on plays like this one. And in that event I shall be in Surbiton too, I hope.

**Chairman** We seem to be getting away from the play itself. Can we try to reach agreement on what kind of production this is? Is it a comedy? The play has a sub-title – *The Accapictor Michmacted: a Comedy*. Denzil Pepper – what do you think about this play as a comedy?

**Pepper** What do I think about it as a comedy? I believe I laughed once. So, technically, I suppose the play could be called a comedy.

**Mrs Vinegar** As a matter of curiosity – what was it Denzil Pepper laughed at?

**Pepper** I really can't remember what it was.

**Mustard** Perhaps calling it a comedy is part of the comedy?

**Pepper** Perhaps so. If someone had told me that, I would certainly have done what I could to laugh. But that's just what I'm never quite sure about – what *is* it we're being asked to do here? Are we being asked to laugh at him, laugh with him – or are we meant, God forbid, to take him seriously?

**Mustard**  It's satire, surely.

**Miss Salt**  What was it Swift called satire? A mirror, wasn't it, in which a man sees any face but his own. It's certainly very true here.

**Mustard**  'Satire is a sort of glass, wherein beholders do generally discover everybody's face but their own.'

**Pepper**  I would have been delighted to have caught a glimpse even of my own face!

**Miss Salt**  Oh, the face was there. It was impossible at times to identify it, even to distinguish it – it will take a careful reading and re-reading of the play to do that – but the face was there. Of that I'm quite certain.

**Chairman**  Did you, Mustard Short, discover a face you could recognise?

**Mustard**  None, I'm afraid. None whatever.

**Miss Salt**  A contorted face, perhaps? I thought I saw that. The human face. In the human predicament. Contorted with grief? With pain?

**Mrs Vinegar**  With boredom.

**Mustard**  Could he, I wonder, be satirising satire?

**Chairman**  A skit on satire itself. How does that strike you, Miss Salt?

**Miss Salt**  Yes. Yes, I think it very likely. I'm wondering whether perhaps rather than 'skit' the word 'parody' would hit off better what it is he's trying for here. Could he be parodying the whole thing? The whole concept? A parody *of* a skit, if that's possible.

**Pepper**  If this is a parody of a skit at all, it must be a parody of a skit *on* something.

**Mustard** A parody of a skit on satire?

**Pepper** For a sophisticated audience. It goes without saying that it's a sophisticated audience he's got in mind here. I take it that's agreed.

**Mustard** A sophisticated audience .

**Mrs Vinegar** A sophisticated audience flagging.

**Mustard** No. I think, if I may say so, Mrs Vinegar is being rather too uncompromisingly hostile to what is – let us be as fair as we possibly can about it – to what is by any standards a remarkable . . . a remarkable phenomenon.

**Miss Salt** I'd rather like to take up this idea of the skit again, or the parody of it, because – and this is surely the whole point which none of us has made yet – here is a play in which the writer is imitating himself repeatedly all through the play. He is in fact actually burlesquing his own self-mimicry and in quite the most devastating way from first to last. That I think is inherent in the whole thing.

**Pepper** He's satirising farce, of course, too. That comes across quite unmistakably. As one of the characters says somewhere in the play – this is the custard-pie farce of the intellect.

**Mustard** Comedy. Custard-pie comedy. Of the abstract. But to get back to this point about burlesque. It is, basically, a parody of a skit on satire that he's burlesquing, and the farce is so to speak a by-product of that. I don't think he's aiming at farce at all. The farce is in a sense what we, the audience, *contribute*.

**Chairman** The audience. Did anyone else, I wonder, feel – as I certainly did – that the barrier between audience and actors was being quite deliberately dismantled? Mrs Vinegar?

**Mrs Vinegar**  It's been done before. And done better.

**Mustard**  You mean the *Verfremdungseffekt*. The alienation effect.

**Miss Salt**  It's Brecht, of course – though with a very different aim from that of Brecht.

**Pepper**  No. I don't see Brecht here at all.

**Miss Salt**  It's the Brechtian technique carried on *beyond* Brecht. Isn't that it?

**Mustard**  Beyond, and in a sense of course at a tangent to Brecht. It's as though he'd gone off on a branch line some way back which is carrying him further than Brecht was able to go but in a quite different direction.

**Miss Salt**  And, of course, *facing* Brecht as he moves away from him. The farther he goes *beyond* Brecht, therefore, the farther he is retreating *from* him.

**Pepper**  I can accept Brecht as starting point. But a starting point is something you move away from, and in my view the author of this play has been doing just that. He has been putting more and more ground between himself and his model – if that's what Brecht is, though I doubt it – and they have been getting farther and farther apart, these two, until both of them are specks on the horizon. Which is why I think we're quite wrong to be discussing this play or whatever it is as if it were *The Comedy of Errors* rewritten by Lewis Carroll to provide a part for Godot or somebody.

**Chairman**  Yes. Well, now our time is running out and I think we ought to say something about the ending – which we've none of us yet seen of course. Is it possible that some of the shortcomings of the play so far could be redeemed by the ending? Mrs Vinegar?

**Mrs Vinegar** I doubt whether I could sit through any more of it. I have never begrudged danger money to steeplejacks and people of that kind, and I do think it's high time someone suggested boredom money for critics. The ending? No. I think the piece is beyond redemption. The best that can be hoped for from the ending is that sooner or later it will arrive.

**Chairman** Denzil Pepper. What do you think about the ending?

**Pepper** I think it's the Russians, isn't it, who have a proverb to the effect that if you can't hold a horse by the mane, you'll never hold it by the tail?

*Pause.*

**Mustard** You can count all the same on being dragged a reasonable distance before having to let go.

**Pepper** Possibly. I'm not sure, though, that I want to do my travelling at the tail of a runaway horse.

**Mrs Vinegar** Is it travelling along the road of life we're talking about? Because as far as that journey is concerned, I broke the back of it this evening during the first act.

**Chairman** And that I'm afraid will have to end the discussion if not the play, because our time is up. I'm sorry to have to apply the guillotine to a discussion which has been so lively – I think we've rarely had a livelier discussion of any play. And a play which can stimulate as much strong feeling, or even boredom –

*Laughter.*

– is something we can always do with in the theatre. I'm sure we would all of us agree, whatever our individual reactions to it may have been, that we have here a play the real author of which will not be born for many years to come.

**All** Hear, hear.

*The light in the living room fades. A half-light reveals the author's mouthpiece, who is sitting on a chair staring ahead with a quite blank expression. He starts convulsively, stands up and looks, with no change of expression, towards the audience. As the lights come up in the living room, revealing Bro Paradock sitting with a newspaper before him, the author's mouthpiece glances quickly in that direction, and then goes slowly out as though dazed.*

*The scene is exactly the same as in Act One, Scene One. Middie Paradock comes into the room and begins tidying it, speaking as she does so.*

**Mrs Paradock** There's somebody at the door wanting you to form a government.

**Mr Paradock** When?

**Mrs Paradock** He says he's working through the street directory. He's waiting outside now.

**Mr Paradock** What does he look like?

**Mrs Paradock** In an old raincoat. He's probably trying it on. I shall want this cork opened in case we have to offer him a drink.

**Mr Paradock** It's nectar if it's anything. Not ambrosia.

**Mrs Paradock** He won't be able to tell the difference.

**Mr Paradock** If he can't tell the difference between ambrosia and nectar he shouldn't be wearing an old raincoat.

**Mrs Paradock** He's only trying it on for size. I got that much out of him.

**Mr Paradock** In that case what does he want me to form a government for?

**Mrs Paradock**  I should have thought that was obvious.

**Mr Paradock**  Supposing it turns out to be Uncle Ted having a joke?

**Mrs Paradock**  You know as well as I do Uncle Ted hasn't got a sense of humour any longer.

**Mr Paradock**  He may think I look like Gladstone.

**Mrs Paradock**  What if he does? You've got a good many years in front of you yet.

**Mr Paradock**  Don't start on that, Middie, please.

**Mrs Paradock**  You're in your prime.

**Mr Paradock**  Middie!

**Mrs Paradock**  A man with your constitution at your time of life is in for a good long spell of it yet.

**Mr Paradock**  Can't you leave me alone, Middie? Can't you keep quiet about it?

**Mrs Paradock**  You're as fit as you've ever been.

**Mr Paradock**  Stop baiting me, Middie! Just shut up about being in my prime. You only keep on about it because you know it plays merry hell with my death wish!

*Blackout. Enter, in front of living room set, a Man in a Bowler Hat carrying a manuscript case.*

**Man in Bowler Hat**  Who's in charge here? Where's the producer or somebody?

*Enter Producer from right.*

They've had about as much as they can take of this out there. (*To audience.*) I don't know how you feel about my breaking in on the production like this, but – (*To Producer.*) I think we've all had about enough.

**Producer** You think the curtain ought to come down, sir?

**Man in Bowler Hat** It's unpleasant for everyone when an audience begins to get restive. (*To audience.*) I know that only too well from an experience of my own when I was foolish enough on one occasion to consent to act as chairman at a political meeting, of all things. The member was speaking – or rather not the member, because as it turned out he lost his deposit – but the candidate, as he was then, was speaking at the time and some unruly elements . . .

*Enter from right Author in high spirits.*

**Author** Well. What a waste of talent it's all been! What a waste!

**Man in Bowler Hat** (*in sotto voce panic*) *Pas devant les auditeurs!*

**Author** *Les auditeurs.* I must say they've all for the most part taken insult after insult in a splendid spirit. Don't you think so?

**Producer** They've taken it very well. But I think perhaps we ought to try and get the curtain down. They'll be wanting to get away.

**Author** I'll have a little chat with them. Take Henry Irving with you and get working on the curtain – it's probably jammed.

*Producer and Man in Bowler Hat go out right.*

It's been an odd evening to say the least of it. I don't quite know whether it would be arrogant of me to take the blame on the grounds that it was I who initiated it all – or whether perhaps we ought all to share bouquets and brickbats promiscuously among us. My own contribution probably seems more important than it is because, as I say, it was my small contribution which set it all going, as it were – and yet, if it comes to that, which of you with a shot or two of benzedrine couldn't have done as well or better? But there is an important point which may be overlooked unless I draw attention to it now and it's this: the retreat from reason means precious little to anyone who has never caught up with reason in the first place. It takes a trained mind to relish a *non sequitur*. So you can take comfort from that. And now one last thing. This is a delicate subject to broach but . . . we on this side of the footlights feel that some gesture from us would be more than appropriate in view of . . . of your forbearance, but on the other hand we felt that anything we might do by way of applauding the audience would seem somehow to smack if not of affectation at any rate of . . . the unconventional? We don't want to fly in the face of tradition but . . .

> *Lights come up in the living room set where the cast is assembled. Each holds a glass of a bright, purple liquid ready to respond to a toast.*

The audience!

**All** The audience!

> *They drink.*

> *Curtain.*

# GLADLY OTHERWISE

# Characters

**Mrs Brandywine**
**Mr Brandywine**
**Man**

*Scene: an ordinary living room.*

*Mr Brandywine sits in a backless chair at one side of the
stage with his back to the other characters. He is probably
over forty, but otherwise of indeterminate age; he is
wearing a dark jacket from one suit and trousers which
more or less match from another. A wig conceals a
completely bald head. He can be reading a small paperback
book, but is quite motionless throughout – more like
a human doorstop than anything else. Mrs Brandywine is
a woman in her early forties, whose manner has a sort
of surface equanimity which may well conceal hidden
depths of neurosis. She has on a good plain grey dress.
She sits with her back to both her husband and the door;
she is sorting through a number of what appear to be
quarto-size photographs until she holds up one for
inspection at arm's length which is seen to be a full-sized
handprint, such as a palmist might find useful. She starts
up at the sound of a voice off. It is full of booming
resonance. It belongs to a Man with a briefcase, who,
when he appears, is large and dominant and may well be
a salesman. If not, then he is in all probability either a
practitioner of psychiatric hypnotism or a trade unionist
turned marriage guidance counsellor. Failing this, he
can only be a rent collector without portfolio. At all
events, he is brisk and in control throughout, and at his
most disquieting when least emphatic. He catches Mrs
Brandywine on the wrong foot at the outset and thwarts
every attempt she makes to regain her balance by tilting
the ground under her whenever she seems to have steadied
herself.*

**Man** (*off*) Mrs Brandywine?

*Mrs Brandywine starts up. The Man enters.*

In here, is it? Ah – there you are, Mrs Brandywine.

**Mrs Brandywine** (*at a loss*) Good morning.

**Man** (*tapping the door handle*) How are your handles? Fit the hand, do they? More or less?

**Mrs Brandywine** (*hesitant*) Yes. Yes – I should say they do. On the whole.

**Man** Good.

*He stands back a pace or two from the door and casts a professional eye at the handle.*

What are they like to look at?

**Mrs Brandywine** To what?

**Man** (*glancing up at her*) When you look at them, do they give you any particular feeling? Revulsion? Contempt? Anything of that sort? Nausea?

**Mrs Brandywine** Not in the ordinary way. No, I can't say they do.

*The Man turns abruptly and crosses to the table, uninvited, where he sets down his briefcase and begins to open it.*

**Man** You see, handles are funny things, Mrs Brandywine. You don't mind if I come in a moment? These aren't my outdoor shoes and the sooner I get inside . . .

**Mrs Brandywine** Of course not. Come in.

**Man** Thank you very much, Mrs. Brandywine. A cup of tea would be very welcome if you could manage it.

**Mrs Brandywine** (*flustered still*) Yes. I've got one outside.

*Mrs Brandywine exits.*

**Man** It's nearly four hours since I had anything.

*Mrs Brandywine reappears.*

**Mrs Brandywine** Hot or cold?

**Man** (*taking papers out of his briefcase and closing it; without looking up*) Depends entirely on the temperature, Mrs Brandywine.

*Mrs Brandywine goes out again. The Man surveys the room, examining handles. Mrs Brandywine returns with a cup of tea.*

I've been looking at your handles, Mrs Brandywine.

*Mrs Brandywine sets down a teacup and saucer, and begins to recover her composure.*

**Mrs Brandywine** Do you like them?

**Man** Very nice. A present from someone, I expect.

**Mrs Brandywine** No, not really.

**Man** Keepsake, perhaps – eh? Former lover? Childhood sweetheart?

**Mrs Brandywine** Good gracious, no. There's no secret about those.

**Man** Oh?

**Mrs Brandywine** They were there when we came.

**Man** But how did they get there, Mrs Brandywine?

*Mrs Brandywine is brought up short by this question, and keeps a very precarious hold on her poise during the following colloquy.*

Two handles on each door – one on either side. They didn't come there by accident.

**Mrs Brandywine**  I've never really thought about it, to tell you the truth.

**Man**  I'm asking you to think about it now, Mrs Brandywine.

**Mrs Brandywine**  Unless the builder put them there.

**Man**  I see.

**Mrs Brandywine**  For some reason.

**Man**  What else was he responsible for?

**Mrs Brandywine**  What else?

**Man**  The builder. Besides the handles.

**Mrs Brandywine**  Oh. Well, everything really. Oh, yes – he was very good.

**Man**  (*looking at her*) I see.

**Mrs Brandywine**  Made all the arrangements. I didn't have to do a thing. Doors, windows, ceilings.

**Man**  Took complete charge, in other words.

**Mrs Brandywine**  Yes. I left it entirely to him, I'm afraid.

**Man**  Chimneys?

**Mrs Brandywine**  Chimneys. Roof. Drains. *I* wouldn't have known where to start. But he seemed to have it all organised.

**Man**  You were reasonably satisfied, were you? On the whole?

**Mrs Brandywine**  Very much so.

**Man**  Plumbing?

**Mrs Brandywine**  Oh, yes.

**Man**  No snags there?

**Mrs Brandywine**  Not that I could see. We had pipes, and outlets for the water. Bath upstairs. Everything – even down to the washers on the taps. And plugs, for the washbasins.

**Man**  He seems to have thought of everything.

**Mrs Brandywine**  Quite honestly we should have been lost without him.

**Man**  What did he charge you?

**Mrs Brandywine**  I really can't remember now. I expect he put a bit on the bill – but whatever it was, I didn't begrudge a penny.

**Man**  I'm sure you didn't. (*He peers out through a window.*) How far can you see through these windows?

**Mrs Brandywine**  It depends, really.

**Man**  What are these? Shelves?

**Mrs Brandywine**  Some are shelves. Some are ledges.

**Man**  Getting proper support from them?

**Mrs Brandywine**  Oh, yes. I can't complain.

**Man**  I'm not asking you to complain, Mrs Brandywine.

**Mrs Brandywine**  I'm more than satisfied with them, actually.

**Man**  Recesses go back far enough?

**Mrs Brandywine**  Just right, really.

**Man**  Not too deep?

**Mrs Brandywine**  Oh, no.

**Man**  Nice upright walls.

**Mrs Brandywine**  Oh, yes. They're very vertical.

**Man** (*looking round the room*) I don't see the floor anywhere.

**Mrs Brandywine** It's under the carpet.

**Man** Making full use of it, I hope.

**Mrs Brandywine** It's just so that we've got something to walk about on, really.

**Man** What length are your floorboards?

**Mrs Brandywine** I'll get a tape measure.

*She finds one in a drawer, but never gets round to using it.*

**Man** Wallpaper? That seems to be missing.

**Mrs Brandywine** We've had it all pushed back against the wall.

**Man** (*looking first at the wall, then significantly at Mrs Brandywine*). Why have you done that, Mrs Brandywine?

**Mrs Brandywine** It gives us more space. In the middle.

**Man** Space?

**Mrs Brandywine** In case we have people in.

**Man** What sort of people?

**Mrs Brandywine** I can tell you better when they've been, really.

**Man** I'd rather you told me now, Mrs Brandywine.

**Mrs Brandywine** People vary so.

**Man** You could give me a rough idea.

**Mrs Brandywine** Well . . .

**Man** Total strangers? Friends of the family? Horsemen of the Apocalypse?

**Mrs Brandywine** It's hard to say. I suppose some of them might be.

**Man** And the others?

**Mrs Brandywine** I'd only be guessing.

**Man** Laundry workers, perhaps?

**Mrs Brandywine** I just couldn't say till I've seen them.

*The Man goes dubiously back to the table where he sits down to fill in the questionnaire he took out of his briefcase earlier.*

**Man** (*looking up in a disenchanted way*) Where are your colanders?

**Mrs Brandywine** (*a little anxious to make amends*) There's one in the kitchen.

*She makes tentatively for the door.*

**Man** Plenty of holes?

**Mrs Brandywine** Oh, yes. Any amount.

**Man** (*stopping short*). *Any* amount?

**Mrs Brandywine** It's chock-a-block with holes.

*The Man continues looking at her.*

I don't know what to do with them sometimes. (*A little wildly.*) I'm falling over them. There's just too many. You don't need all that many. There's no room for anything else.

**Man** You don't know the exact number?

**Mrs Brandywine** Not offhand. I'm afraid I don't.

**Man** (*returning to the form*) Sieves all letting the small stuff through?

**Mrs Brandywine**  So far, touch wood.

*The Man makes one or two jottings, puts the paper back in his briefcase and seems to relax. His eye as he does this is caught by a tea cosy knitted in bright colours. He momentarily interrupts himself to pick it up, comment and put it down again.*

**Man**  Pretty.

**Mrs Brandywine**  Do you like it?

**Man**  Attractive colours.

**Mrs Brandywine**  It's a tea cosy.

**Man**  Did you knit it, Mrs Brandywine?

**Mrs Brandywine**  I did and I didn't, really.

**Man**  Had an accomplice, very likely.

**Mrs Brandywine**  I wouldn't call it that exactly.

**Man**  Why not, Mrs Brandywine?

**Mrs Brandywine**  Unless you call Mrs Prebabel an accomplice.

**Man**  What's wrong with calling her Mrs Prebabel?

**Mrs Brandywine**  Oh, nothing at all.

**Man**  It's her name presumably?

**Mrs Brandywine**  Oh, yes.

**Man**  Not an alias, or anything of that sort?

**Mrs Brandywine**  Oh, no. It's her proper name. She married a Mr Prebabel.

**Man**  Then why are you asking me to call her an accomplice, Mrs Brandywine?

**Mrs Brandywine**  It's just that she helped me with the tea cosy.

**Man** Oh?

**Mrs Brandywine** (*becoming a little wild again*) She held the needles. I looked after the wool.

**Man** I see.

**Mrs Brandywine** We were in it together, as you might say.

**Man** In other words you were just as much an accomplice as Mrs Prebabel was?

**Mrs Brandywine** If you put it like that, I suppose I was.

> *Pause, during which the Man looks intently at Mrs Brandywine before changing course. He closes his briefcase with a snap, takes it up and makes for the door.*

**Man** (*speaking without looking at her*) Not always very sure of yourself, are you, Mrs Brandywine?

**Mrs Brandywine** Oh . . .

**Man** Some of your answers could come a little more pat.

> *He checks on seeing Mr Brandywine for the first time and goes towards him inquisitively.*

You should try to get a lot more glibness into your whole approach. (*Looking back at her.*) This is new.

**Mrs Brandywine** It's my husband.

**Man** (*looking him over from various angles*) Everything functioning?

**Mrs Brandywine** Oh, yes.

> *The Man lifts Mr Brandywine's wig to reveal a totally bald head.*

**Man** (*accusingly*) Except his hormones.

**Mrs Brandywine** I've tried everything.

**Man** What does he weigh?

**Mrs Brandywine** Naked?

**Man** Dressed.

**Mrs Brandywine** Eleven stone twelve.

**Man** (*trying the chair with his foot*) The chair's taking most of that.

**Mrs Brandywine** He manages on what's left.

**Man** (*about to go*) Is he serving any purpose? Sitting there?

**Mrs Brandywine** (*wildly trying to be more glib*) Only to keep the floorboards in position.

**Man** (*in a tone of grave reproof*) There are nails for that, Mrs Brandywine.

*Mrs Brandywine is at a loss.*

(*Going.*) You could dispense with one or the other. You don't need both. (*Checking.*) What are his kidneys like?

**Mrs Brandywine** (*as before*) He never lets me see them.

**Man** You could wait till he's gone out.

**Mrs Brandywine** I don't like to rummage behind his back.

**Man** It's in his own interests, Mrs Brandywine.

*The Man goes out. Mrs Brandywine turns away, bemused, and notices the full cup of tea.*

**Mrs Brandywine** (*calling*) You haven't drunk your tea.

**Man** (*off*) I prefer to see it in the cup. (*More distant.*) I'll be in touch with you, Mrs Brandywine. As soon as anything comes through.

*Mrs Brandywine sits down. She shrugs off the episode and is herself again. All the same, she is too preoccupied to return to the album. Mr Brandywine looks up from his reading and turns his head to look at Mrs Brandywine, who has her back to him. He turns back, half turns his head and speaks without looking at her.*

**Mr Brandywine** (*nodding sharply towards the door*) Relative?

**Mrs Brandywine** (*returning sharply to the album as she answers with unemphatic asperity*) He didn't say.

*Mr Brandywine returns to his book. The scene is exactly as at the beginning. There is a tableau for less than a second.*